UNDERCURRENTS

Defending Peace: Ireland's Role in
a Changing Europe

UNDERCURRENTS

Other titles in the series

Facing the Unemployment Crisis in Ireland by Kieran Kennedy

Divorce in Ireland: Who Should Bear the Cost? by Peter Ward

Crime and Crisis in Ireland: Justice by Illusion? by Caroline Fennell

The Hidden Tradition: Feminism, Women and Nationalism in Ireland by Carol Coulter

Managing the EU Structural Funds in Ireland by Alan Matthews

Diverse Communities: The Evolution of Lesbian and Gay Politics in Ireland by Kieran Rose

Democracy Blindfolded: The Case for a Freedom of Information Act in Ireland by Patrick Smyth and Ronan Brady

Ireland: The Emigrant Nursery and the World Economy by Jim MacLaughlin

Women and the New Reproductive Technologies in Ireland by Susan Ryan-Sheridan

Travellers and Ireland: Whose Country, Whose History? by Jim MacLaughlin

Rethinking the War on Drugs in Ireland by Tim Murphy

Last Rights: Death, Dying and the Law in Ireland by Patrick Hanafin

Prison Policy in Ireland: Criminal Justice versus Social Justice by Paul O'Mahony

Farm Incomes: Myths and Reality by Alan Matthews

Refugees and Asylum-Seekers in Ireland by Paul Cullen

The Politics of Children's Rights by Frank Martin

Understanding Political Corruption in Irish Politics by Neil Collins and Mary O'Shea

Crime Control in Ireland: The Politics of Intolerance by Ian O'Donnell and Eoin O'Sullivan

A Judgment too far? Judicial Activism and the Constitution by David Gwynn Morgan

UNDERCURRENTS   Series Editor Carol Coulter

Defending Peace: Ireland's Role in a Changing Europe

JOHN MAGUIRE

CORK UNIVERSITY PRESS

First published in 2002 by
Cork University Press
University College
Cork
Ireland

© John Maguire 2002

All rights reserved. No part of this book may be reprinted
or reproduced or utilized in any electronic, mechanical or other
means, now known or hereafter invented, including photocopying and
recording or otherwise, without either the prior written permission
of the Publishers or a licence permitting restricted copying in
Ireland issued by the Irish Copyright Licensing Agency Ltd,
The Irish Writers' Centre, 19 Parnell Square, Dublin 1.

The author has asserted his moral right in this work.

British Library Cataloguing in Publication Data
A CIP catalogue record for this book is available from
the British Library

ISBN 1 85918 357 3

Typeset by Tower Books, Ballincollig, Co. Cork
Printed by ColourBooks, Baldoyle, Co. Dublin

Further informaton on topics discussed in this essay can be obtained from Afri (Action for Ireland) www.afri.buz.org, and from other organisations indicated in the bibliography.

This essay is dedicated,
with gratitude and respect,
to the late
Raymond Crotty
and the late
Erskine Childers III

Contents

Preface	ix
Glossary	xv
Introduction	1
The Options before us: The Core Argument	3
War and Contemporary Society	6
War and Its Impact	6
Words, Deeds and Meanings	7
Defence, Democracy and Delegation	9
War in the Contemporary World	13
Thinking the Unfashionable: From Offence to Defence	22
Democratizing Democracy	25
Irish Foreign Policy: the European Context	31
Obligations to our European Friends	31
Ireland, Europe and the Wider World	32
The US and World Security	35
Before 11 September 2001	36
After 11 September	39
The United Nations	43
The Framing of the United Nations	45
Dirty Work at the Crossroads: 'Desert Storm' to Kosovo	48
The UN: Last Best Hope or Ultimate Delusion?	52
Kofi Annan Interview and Editorial	57
Letting Slip the Dogs of War	63
Our Politicians and Neutrality	63
SEA/Maastricht/Amsterdam: EU Military Policy Evolves	66
A Broken Promise: Ireland Joins NATO/PfP	71

viii   CONTENTS

NATO goes to War: the Lessons of Kosovo   73

Peace Process or 'War on Terrorism'?   84

Hope Comes at Last: East Timor's Coalition of the Willing   101

That was Nice: Let's do it Again!   106
   Nice and a European Army?   107
   We Don't Heed no Declaration: We Demand
      A Protocol!   114
   Nice, Peace and Democracy: An Unlikely Trio? 122

Restating Neutrality: Building a Safer World   125

Bibliography   131

Preface

The chief aim of this essay is to persuade my fellow-citizens of the need to challenge the EU's evolving military structures, as provided for most recently in the Nice Treaty. The potential consequences of lethal military force require transparent democratic accountability, which is seriously lacking in the EU structures. The issue of democracy has been widened and deepened by the Irish government's reaction to losing the Nice debate in the 2001 referendum: they have attempted to deflect people's concerns about the Treaty, as these are interpreted by the government itself, whilst insisting that the Treaty text can in no circumstances be revisited. This sharply focuses our disquiet about the lack of democracy in Irish and EU decision-making, which disquiet is heightened in turn by a consideration of certain other, also allegedly non-negotiable, contents of Nice.

If the government have been far from transparent in their handling of issues of substance, they have been all too transparent in their attempts to re-brand the Nice Treaty; having once lost the argument, they have now decided 'if we can't win it, we'll spin it'. This is most apparent in the claim that the treaty is indispensable for EU enlargement, which the EU Commission President amongst others has contradicted. The decision to manipulate enlargement to browbeat the Irish electorate has put the enlargement project itself quite unnecessarily at risk, whilst handing to all comers a detailed script, written by our own government, for caricaturing the Irish electorate as irresponsible and ungenerous.

This tendency to tell us ever more insistently what EU treaties are 'really' about, rather than to answer our actual questions about them, has long been at work in relation to the EU's evolving military apparatus. It goes along with the dismissal of anyone who remains unconvinced as an uninformed, probably dishonest 'nay-sayer'. This represents a stubborn and undemocratic refusal to accept that there is a large and growing constituency of people, positively and clear-sightedly committed to genuine peace building under direct UN authority, who see our entanglement with the evolving EU military structure as competing with and undermining, rather than complementing and enhancing, that commitment.

We are told that the European policy is benign, whereas it is influenced by, and legally obliged to be compatible with, the aggressive doctrines of NATO's nuclear alliance. We are told that it is mainly about humanitarian relief and peacekeeping, whereas it incorporates vague and open-ended military tasks including 'peacemaking', that is actual combat in the name of peace. We are told that all of this is compatible with international law and the United Nations, whereas the policy is not subject to direct UN authority. Moreover the EU, including Ireland, has already endorsed NATO's illegal bombing over Kosovo, based on the clearly false claim that every alternative means of conflict resolution had been tried and failed.

All of these developments are presented as inevitable, because the United Nations, we are told, has insufficient resources for full-spectrum peace building, lacks the requisite authority, and increasingly relies on 'regional bodies' such as NATO. It can however be shown that the countries promoting this negative view of the UN are in fact leading NATO members, who have crafted the lack of UN resources and authority which they then exploit and hypocritically bemoan. A reclaimed and revitalised UN is the only forum which can make a reality of those values of peaceful conflict resolution, subjecting any necessary use of minimal force to international law, which our governments continue to proclaim but have served ill by their silence and evasion while EU military forces have evolved.

Opponents of current EU military policy, far from 'naysaying', are positively committed to the creative restatement, in today's circumstances, of the values expressed in Ireland's long, proud and effective role of UN peacekeeping. To do this will involve confronting the current conventional wisdom which equates 'defence' unthinkingly with aggressive militarism, as well as the hugely destructive arms trade in which Ireland is becoming increasingly incorporated, partly as a direct result of our membership of the EU Rapid Reaction Force. The contemporary military policies and structures in which we are being urged to 'play our part' are a major cause of the problems of poverty and conflict to which they then offer themselves as the solution.

Whilst our foreign policy could never claim the 'holier-than-thou' status so often imputed by its detractors, it did embody a sense of our historical experience and our place in the world, which led us in the 1950s and 1960s especially to take worthwhile stances on issues such as nuclear disarmament and UN peacekeeping. This gave us a profile, in the eyes of more recently liberated former colonies, as a western country not totally absorbed in wealthy big-power politics. That profile has been sadly and unnecessarily eroded by our failure to uphold our principles, and creatively restate our traditional values, in our dealings with our EU colleagues and with the United States. The result is that we have acquiesced in structures and actions, for example in the 'War on Terrorism', which are seriously at odds with the basis of our peace process, in which the US, the UK and other EU colleagues themselves have played key roles.

We have too often allowed the risk of being smeared as 'anti-European' or 'anti-American' prevent us from speaking truth to our friends. Our failure to establish adult relationships with our neighbours and friends means that we are now confronted with a challenge, whether to go along with militaristic structures or to use our confidence and resources to help build a more peaceful and less militarised world. Having failed to articulate such a position while EU common military structures emerged, our government is reduced to promoting them in purely negative terms, by reassuring us how little we need to be committed to them. We are also told that they do not endanger neutrality, which latter however is defined purely in terms of military alliance, and this in turn pared down to the issue of a mutual defence obligation.

The declarations made at Seville in June 2002 by the EU and the Irish government, apparently designed to put our minds at rest on military issues, actually sharpen our concerns. The very fact of obtaining two separate declarations underlines our failure to convince our EU colleagues of basic values such as the effective primacy of the UN. In any case, being merely statements *about* rather than *in* the treaty text, they have no binding legal force. They are no more reliable than the government promise to hold a referendum on joining NATO's 'Partnership for Peace', which was jettisoned as soon as legal advice was obtained that it was not legally binding. The government claims to have gone one better than the declarations, with its proposal to add a provision about a possible single European army to the question put in an autumn referendum. Not only is a second referendum on an unchanged Nice Treaty democratically improper and arguably unconstitutional; the proposed wording is also of limited benefit at best. Even if it would, as claimed, provide for us to approve a 'common European defence' without having to be part of it, this does nothing to repair the damage already done by our entanglement in a common European offence: it is concerned purely with a possible issue for the future, rather than with the present reality and corrosive effects of the European Rapid Reaction Force.

In contemplating a second Nice referendum, and in discussing the future of the EU over the next few years, there is the possibility of a real debate. If the establishment are right, then the concerns being voiced over Nice and other matters come from an intellectually dishonest bunch of whingeing nay-sayers who will never be reassured because they want never to be reassured. Alternatively, what is happening is that the electorate are at last beginning to question the actual content of EU treaties, rather than simply following instructions to take the money (if there is any) and vote on the dotted line. This, if properly responded to, can only be healthy for Irish democracy and for the democracy of the EU, in its present form and as it enlarges.

* * *

I wish to acknowledge the substantial contribution of Afri (Action from Ireland), with the support of the Joseph Rowntree Charitable Trust, towards the costs of publishing this book, and also the additional help of Comhlámh. I am very grateful to the immensely efficient and helpful staff of Cork University Press. I have also received help and encouragement, of various kinds, from a large number of people. I must particularly thank Tom Dunne for his crucial support in so many ways. Joe Noonan, as always, has helped me indispensably with his comments on drafts and with his generous encouragement. Joe Murray and Andy Storey have helped by comments on drafts and with a vast range of support that is hugely appreciated. I am grateful to members and staff of Comhlámh in Cork, and to many others, whose names I hope I have fully listed here: Thomas Bieler, Edward Burke, Geraldine Campbell, Ken Coates, Nikki Darrell, Mark Doris, Valerie Fletcher, Mary Foley, Carol Fox, Kathy Glavanis Grantham, John Goodwillie, Mary Linehan, Piaras MacEinri, Marianne Moore, Clare O'Grady Walshe, Clare O'Halloran, Andrew O'Riordan, Michael Quane, Tony Simpson, and various officials of the Departments of Defence and of Foreign Affairs, of the National Forum on Europe and of the UN. Lastly, my thanks to Sarah for the surfing, Úna for the books, and both of them for their constant warmth and encouragement.

All the views expressed in this essay are of course my own responsibility.

John Maguire
Cork, July 2002

Glossary

Afri:	Action from Ireland
EEC:	European Economic Community
ENPHR:	European Network for Peace and Human Rights
ERRF:	European Rapid Reaction Force
ETISC:	East Timor Ireland Solidarity Campaign
EU:	European Union
IICK:	Independent International Commission on Kosovo
NATO:	North Atlantic Treaty Organization
NATO/PfP:	NATO's 'Partnership for Peace'
OSCE:	Organization for Security and Co-operation in Europe
PANA:	Peace and Neutrality Alliance
QMV:	Qualified (i.e., weighted) majority voting
SEA:	Single European Act
UNAMIR:	United Nations Assistance Mission for Rwanda
UNPROFOR:	United Nations Protection Force
UNSAS:	United Nations Standby Arrangements System
WEU:	Western European Union

Note: I have used the spelling al-Qa'ida, although respecting the alternative spelling al-Qaeda in quotations.

Introduction

Ireland is faced with some crucial questions in relation to defence and security. We face issues such as the shape to be given to defence and security policy in the evolving EU; what relation this will have to NATO and the Western European Union (WEU), and how we in Ireland will relate to these developments. These questions arise in a new and very challenging context. The end of the Cold War left a world with only one 'superpower', and a set of military arrangements, particularly in NATO, which needed to be rethought. We also have a heightened awareness of massacres and pogroms such as those in Rwanda and the former Yugoslavia, and of the need for a decent, helpful response to them. Most recently, there have been the atrocities of 11 September 2001 in the USA, with all their complex and evolving consequences.

It is striking, having written an earlier version of this argument some three years ago, how radically things have changed in that short span. In 1999 there were problems and challenges aplenty, and much urgency; yet there was also a sense of some space and time for reflection and for choice. Now, the world seems to be heading, at a dizzying pace, towards the seeming certainties of war and all the uncertainties and horrors that it brings. There is a sense that anything spoken or written today might be made redundant by tomorrow's, let alone next year's, events.

Yet this is precisely the time for clarity, particularly in a country like ours that has put much effort and sacrifice into staking out its own space and identity in matters military. There is a palpable sense that we could all choose the path of death and destruction, the culture and practice of war. The questions that hang over that practice, however, are intensified rather than stifled by the press of events: the fog of war should not cast its shadow over our policy.

For many years now there has been a body of opinion that Ireland's only proper response to the contemporary world is to abandon its long-held stance on defence policy; we should, it is argued, 'get involved' and 'play our part', and we can use our influence positively within the new context. I believe that the thinking behind this advice is seriously wrong, and specifically that we should not endorse closer involvement in the emerging European military structures.

I believe that if we examine the case properly we will actually be led in the opposite direction. My immediate aim is to convince the reader that there is a strong case for not continuing along the road which we have travelled, in the past 15 years, of integration into the emerging 'European security architecture'. This would give pause to a deeply flawed and highly dangerous process. Far from simply negating the present course of development, however, we can also contribute to a positive alternative to the militarization of our world.

These questions will be argued out over the coming decade and longer; they also arise sharply in relation to the Nice Treaty. That proposed treaty was negotiated in the context of Ireland's recent accession to NATO's 'Partnership for Peace'. The failure to hold the promised referendum on NATO/PfP means that we have been bundled further down the road of militarism, adding both complexity and urgency to the Nice Treaty decision.

There are some deep-rooted images at work in this debate, influencing what we say and do without being spelt out themselves. One such is a highly negative image of opponents of current policy as unrealistic, nay-sayers, aware more of what they oppose than what they are for, holier-than-thou and irresponsible in wanting to leave necessary evils to others. I believe – unsurprisingly perhaps – that this is a false and unfair picture.

There is a strong case to be made for a new stance against militarism, in a creative restatement of our traditional policy. It is no less informed by reality, less responsible, less positive than the argument I oppose. Of course, neutrality has sometimes served some people as an excuse for irresponsible uninvolvement in issues of peace and security. The solution for that is not to become unthinkingly entangled in structures and commitments that we have not adequately examined.

What I want to do here is to look at some of the basic ideas involved in this debate. I want to look at what kind of rules we think should operate in relation to warfare, and how those rules might best be applied by us. I am trying to clarify the values that both sides in the debate would share, and to see how they can best be realized.

The Options Before Us: the Core Argument

Apart from negative image-making, the argument for military involvement rests on two claims. The first claim is that simply by virtue of EU membership we ought to become involved in developing a common EU defence and security structure or that, because of the benefits we have derived from EU membership, we owe participation in return. The second points to the horrors that have occurred in places such as Rwanda and the former Yugoslavia in the last decade, and the need to prevent such horrors. Hanging over this second argument, since 11 September 2001, is the 'War on Terrorism' with its pressure to play a role in the US-led coalition.

There is an arguable case for what the government and others have been urging on us. It is set out, for example, by Patrick Keatinge and Ben Tonra in *The European Rapid Reaction Force* (2002). This case – which we will examine in detail (see especially pp. 106–121) – is that the EU policy is a relatively modest attempt, along experimental lines, to enhance the capacity of EU member states together to contribute to European and world peace and security.

Those who see anything more (let alone worse) in this are, it seems, misinformed, or misrepresenting the case. Allegedly it is not a military alliance because it does not involve a mutual defence guarantee. Even if there turned out to be anything of sinister significance involved, successive governments have allegedly preserved a number of safeguards against any action contrary to our principles.

That case has but one defect, namely that it is wrong. This essay will argue as follows.

- EU military policy figures in the Nice Treaty, which is an appropriate occasion for us to register our concerns about that policy.
- The ERRF is not a simple stand-alone experiment, but a stage in a process whereby the militaristic assumptions shared by leading EU member states, including key NATO doctrines, have become the basis of the emerging 'European defence identity'.
- Promoters of that identity have been less than candid about the issues at stake, the process of negotiation, and the significance of successive treaties since the Single European Act of 1986/87: the process of negotiation, and interaction with the Irish electorate, has been marked by a lack of clarity at best.
- This process casts doubt on assurances that Irish governments, having prejudiced key principles of our policy while the 'defence identity' emerges, would actually use whatever freedom of decision they claim to have preserved within it.
- A mutual defence obligation is only one of the characteristics of a military alliance, many of which are increasingly evident in the emerging EU structure.
- There are serious grounds to doubt the claim that what is happening is compatible with the traditions and principles, including peacekeeping under the UN, which have informed our policies up to now.
- The central issue at stake, our entanglement in an unacceptable EU military structure, cannot be resolved by any framework of declarations, protocols or constitutional amendments which envisages that entanglement as continuing.
- 'Going along' would represent a huge missed opportunity to implement a radically different and genuine contribution to peace and security.

Behind the events and decisions that confront us, there are always deep and complex *processes* at work (see Glennon, 2001, Ch. 6). Sometimes we mistakenly argue about events and decisions in isolation, overlooking the processes of which they are instances. This happens frequently in the area of defence and security, where for instance new labels like 'peacemaking', proposals for 'rationalization', or policies of 'co-operation' are put forward. Those who question these are then regarded as somehow lacking in understanding, even verging on paranoia: how can they not see how little is involved and/or how much good will come of it?

The real debate concerns the practices and structures – the *processes* – at stake. The question is always how does a proposal arise, in what context, what options does it open up and what does it foreclose? Here, we may isolate at least the following questions.

- What is the process of EU policy formation on security and defence?
- How does this relate to the wider process of EU power and democracy?
- What processes have affected the workings of Western democracies, and global international relations, since the end of the Cold War?
- What processes are at work in the evolution of the United Nations, particularly with respect to groups such as NATO?
- How has Ireland interacted with these developments, and how has that process shaped our foreign policy?

The purpose of this essay is to discuss these questions in the context of the forthcoming 'Nice Referendum mark II' and also in relation to the 2004 EU summit and beyond. The central question concerns the process at work in international relations overall: should we see this as, despite real difficulties, a meaningful process towards peace, or instead as one of accepting war as the answer? We will also briefly consider some related issues, such as the crisis of EU democracy, which have a bearing on any assessment of EU policies.

War and Contemporary Society

War and its Impact

If truth is the first casualty of war, its chief and central casualty is damaged and dead people. Although our culture often shies away from it, we have some realization of the awesomeness of death. This is why we regard murder as a most terrible crime: it puts a stop to someone else's life. Even those of us who are most assured of an afterlife hardly claim the right to dispatch others into it.

An eloquent voice here is that of Bud Welch, whose 27-year-old daughter Julie was killed in the Oklahoma bombing in April 1995. Although going to witness the execution of Timothy McVeigh, he courageously opposed it.

> I will be there, but I won't be waving any placard. The death of this man will be a private moment for me, and a very sad one. I don't think his death is going to help anyone or bring anyone back. (*Observer Magazine*, 22 April 2001)

On the same day in June 2001 on which we were asked to endorse the crystallization of a NATOized EU Rapid Reaction Force, we also faced the decision to remove the death penalty from our Constitution. Those who support the death penalty must face the huge problem of the irreversibility of death.

We have gone some way to thinking out the issue of murder and our attitude to it, but have integrated the realities of warfare far less into our lives. This is implied by Mr Welch's lucid conclusion to his reasoning about Timothy McVeigh: 'If we accept state killing, we accept killing.' Some would carry this logic to the refusal of force even in self-defence, but that is not my position here; I believe people have the right to prevent harm by reasonable means, including minimal force if truly unavoidable.

Yet war is primarily a catastrophic event, designed to destroy people. More than just individual death writ large, it threatens people's very lifeworld; it is the breeding-ground of hatred and revenge. Related to all this is the psychological impact of war and the threat of war: it sows fear deep in the human psyche, restricting our horizons of imagination and justice, silencing our voices. Warfare, by sowing such fear in individuals and populations, destroys the human person insidiously, as do its frequent accomplices, torture and rape. We need to integrate into our thinking the central, huge fact that war is a failure of our species, and each time we engage in it we damage ourselves and our world.

Louie Bennett (1870–1956), one of Ireland's leading suffragists and pacifists throughout the First World War, the independence struggle and the Civil War, asked in 1915:

> Are we right to tolerate in silence this modern warfare, with all its cruelty and waste? ... Let us not blind ourselves with talk of the glories and heroisms of war. We dare not ignore the moral and spiritual wreckages that remain unchronicled. (Cullen Owens, 2001, p. 32)

We have not thought through what force – even defensive force, which Bennett opposed – involves, and what rules should apply to its use.

We think about war as little as possible, perhaps because it is so horrible. There is more of it than we pretend, and it often takes us by surprise. We need to think more often, and more deeply, so that war might happen less often and never overwhelm us. This is one of the chief aims, for example, of the recently launched European Network for Peace and Human Rights: to correct the situation where the peace movement is always the dependent variable, rising and falling tragically with the ebb and flow of war.

Words, Deeds and Meanings

Not only have we an odd approach to war, shutting it out of our daily lives and thinking: as if to compensate, we have done exactly the opposite with our language. We accept the most bellicose vocabulary in day-to-day matters, yet ludicrously sanitize our references to warfare.

Any news bulletin will yield requests for someone to 'spearhead' a new initiative and someone else to 'keep their powder dry', while another will be brought into negotiations to 'knock heads together'. We express geniality by inviting people to 'fire away', while making it quite clear we will 'stick to our guns', try not to be caught by someone else's 'double-edged sword', and avoid 'shooting from the hip' (or 'ourselves in the foot'). Our advertisements, if not prompting a fond smile at a young woman who declares her sister '*so* dead!' for borrowing an item of clothing, invite us to battle-sites in the latest 'price war', or to make a 'killing' in a share flotation.

Our everyday speech has been colonized by the imagery of destruction, most bizarrely by media commentators telling us, with evident relish, how the government plan to 'take no prisoners' in the second Nice referendum. At the same time, our talk of destruction is camouflaged in the most innocent of everyday terms. It is as if we have taken Doctor Strangelove to heart: 'Gentlemen, you can't fight in here: this is the war-room!' When non-combatants suffer, we refer to 'collateral damage'; we speak about 'degrading', rather than 'destroying', an enemy's capacity. There is even an MX missile known as the 'Peacekeeper', while a bomb with local impact equivalent to nuclear weapons is 'the Daisy-cutter'.

One deeply disturbing corruption of language is the ease with which we use the term 'ethnic cleansing'. This 'infamous euphemism' (UN 1999a, p. 109) is a product of insanity, having no objective meaning in the world. We can say 'murder', 'rape', 'torture' and the like meaningfully, because they describe human actions that also are prohibited by law. No human action can be called 'ethnic cleansing', because there are no peoples who are dirt. It speaks volumes about how our minds are parasitic on the culture of violence that we can recycle such an absurdity, undermining any condemnation through deeper connivance with pogroms and mass murder.

Defence, Democracy and Delegation

As well as the abolition of the death penalty, June 2001 also saw a referendum endorse the International Criminal Court by a large majority. This is an important step towards making a reality of international law on conflict. We need greater clarity on the use of force in our name and on how we can ensure that such force does not cause more problems than it cures. When force is used on our behalf we are *delegating* it to a structure, including a professional army.

The more crucial an activity, the more is involved in asking or allowing someone else to do it for us. It is probably a matter of indifference to us who paints our house, or how (so long as exploitation is not involved). What about minding our children? We acknowledge a duty to ensure that the child's experience in our absence will be totally acceptable. What then about teaching our children? The anguish, on all sides, of the recent secondary teachers' disputes has brought home how deep are the questions involved here. They matter so much because the teacher is implementing a choice we make, but cannot fully implement on our own, for our child.

There are many specialist jobs and we can do only a few of them, at the very most, in a lifetime. We would find some of them very hard to do – acting, for example, if we are shy. Then there is an occupation like surgery, which few could do 'from cold': we could not stand the blood and guts. Whatever physical and emotional disgust surgery causes us, we do not usually have a *moral* problem about it; we are glad that enough people acquire this healing skill. We 'delegate' the job to those skilled and tough-minded enough to take it on.

Because of its huge impact, we ensure that medicine is practised under strict conditions by accredited practitioners. There are obvious similarities between being a surgeon and being a soldier. Both require overcoming physical distaste for what one is doing to people. Both are dealing in human life, using dangerous instruments requiring control, precision and timing to succeed. This similarity is driven home when military planners talk about 'surgical strikes'. The image is of swift, skilled, calibrated action designed to restore our health. It is an immensely reassuring image for an immensely disturbing activity, explaining its appeal to those 'selling' warfare to public opinion.

Though we accept the authority of the surgeon, and the strict discipline involved in her or his craft, this extends only to *how* surgery is performed; even then we demand meticulous documentation and a right to legal scrutiny. As regards *whether* surgery will be performed, we have repudiated, at least in principle, the all-knowing authority of the doctor. Surely then, the nearer we approach to planning war, with its deliberate harm and even death, the more open our decision-making should be? Surely we cannot slough off the direct responsibility for force used in our name?

Military force is designed to do harm, however restricted and focused, and is used against the will of the people it is used on, marking it off clearly from surgery. What then of 'patients' rights' in the case of war? We sketch out something equivalent through the Geneva Conventions and other international law. Even these depend on our recognizing that we have to stand in the place of the 'patient', the person – combatant or civilian – on the other side, whose life our actions will affect and may indeed destroy.

Many people sincerely stress the importance of avoiding 'innocent' casualties in warfare. Yet, unless we are committed to the death penalty, we do not believe anyone *deserves* to die. To direct special condemnation at the slaughter of 'the innocent' is understandable, but risks suggesting that the lives of combatants are somehow less valuable or less fully human. The priority should be that there be less violence as such and that it do less harm when it occurs.

The only thing that makes acceptable an action of 'my' army is my moral certainty that I would be prepared in principle to perform that action myself. I may lack the training, confidence and physical courage to perform it, but I must regard it as a right action for me to want to perform. With surgery, for example, we would give consent for an operation on our next-of-kin only if we were morally certain that, if *we* were the surgeon, that is what we would do.

It may be acceptable to regard our soldiers as specialists in physical courage, but we can never hand over to them our moral capacities. My individual conscience is not a luxury which I am too naïve or cowardly to give up; it is a duty towards others, as inalienable as any right ever conceived. War is indeed too terrible to be left to the soldiers, or even to the professional politicians directing them.

We have recently seen a great amount of attention devoted to the tragic death of John Carthy, a young man who was shot by a Garda response team during a disturbed episode at his mother's home in Abbeylara. Quite properly, there has been an investigation. The issues involved have brought an appeal to the Supreme Court and provoked a profound reappraisal of Garda complaints procedures, and the role of the legislature vis-à-vis judicial inquiries. Why do we so casually accept that, in the context of war and as the numbers of dead and injured soar into hundreds or thousands, scrutiny of this type becomes irrelevant?

We have a right to use force to defend ourselves, and a right – sometimes a duty – to use force to defend others as well. But such defensive force must genuinely be a last resort, focused on directly preventing or halting the damage being done. One of the difficulties we meet here is in defining terms: where does stopping someone from doing something bad slide over into preventing them from doing it in the near future, and then to making sure they will not have such a capacity in the longer run?

This very question shows precisely why we have to anchor any action we contemplate in a clear understanding of the true dreadfulness of war. If our focus switches to punishing the wrongdoer as such, or eliminating their capacity to do wrong in the future, then we are entering a spiral of competitive force which sows the seeds of future wars; we are promoting war as a normal practice, rather than viewing defensive strength as something to be called upon only in emergencies.

What then of people who are subjected to conditions of tyrannical oppression? There would be something deeply distasteful in our sitting at ease in prosperous Western Europe, telling the people of South Africa under apartheid, the people of East Timor under Indonesian occupation, or the people of Tibet under Chinese rule, that they may never break the chains of their oppression. Do not those who impose institutional and other violence, which renders political struggle impossible for the oppressed, at some stage become responsible for forceful resistance to themselves?

We can hardly deny the authenticity of, for example, this statement of the Zapatista rebels in southern Mexico:

> We have nothing, absolutely nothing – not decent shelter, nor land, nor work, nor health, nor food, nor education. We do not have the right to choose freely and democratically our officials. We have neither peace nor justice for ourselves and our children. But today we say enough! (Paul Rogers, 1995, p. 1)

In 1965 the UN General Assembly adopted Resolution 2105(XX), which recognizes:

> the legitimacy of the struggle waged by peoples under colonial domination to exercise their right to self-determination and independence. (Tyler and Berry, n.d., p. 35)

Our considerations about force are still relevant – perhaps crucially *more* relevant – in such cases. In other words, it is vitally important to try to avoid creating a new structure and culture of violence. Apart from the distinction between preventing misdeeds and punishing them, there is another consideration which we have already met: the use of force leads to hurt and resentment, and using it beyond the minimum necessary gives a powerful and lasting message that what is needed is to retaliate, next time with greater force; and so the sorry cycle proceeds.

There are areas of life where the right to dissent might be considered (however misguidedly) a luxury; in the area of military policy it is vital. Along with the ultimate right of conscientious objection, we have a right and a duty to prevent our world from becoming objectionable in the first place. I will be told that these conditions are already broadly fulfilled in the democracies. Indeed, some hold that arguments like mine would hamstring the democracies in the face of ruthless dictators and war-mongers who make a mockery of public opinion and free choice.

Here we move from general considerations governing any use of military force to asking how those considerations apply today. There are good reasons to suspect that contemporary 'defence' structures are themselves a key ingredient of the crises for which they claim to be the cure. On the day we voted on Nice and the death penalty, as we have noted, we also ratified the International Criminal Court. Does our practice live up to our promises of respect for international law?

War in the Contemporary World

People might criticize Western approaches to warfare from many viewpoints. Some regret that our zeal for peace and development does not stretch to making real progress in nuclear and non-nuclear disarmament. Others see the current Western approach to the world as a continuation, even an intensification, of previous imperialism. My argument rests on what these two views have in common: the societies with which we are being urged to integrate our defence policy simply do not act like societies whose priority is peace and disarmament.

A real problem confronts anyone trying to address this situation: there are no magic words to utter; they have all been pre-digested by the spin-doctors and PR machines. There are no facts to adduce that have not been gravely nodded over by our leaders, solemnly declaring that 'what *really* matters' is to prevent war from arising in the first place. We face a stark choice: either we accept that competent authorities have things more or less under control or we consider a different and very disturbing possibility, as follows:

The current structure of 'defence' is a vast, self-justifying, aggressive, wasteful and highly dangerous machine, more or less out of control even in democratic societies; we need, not to present ourselves as reliable candidates for promotion within that machine, but to ask the crucial human question: how can the study and practice of peace replace the study and practice of war?

If this claim is true, then those who argue for a 'European defence identity' as currently envisaged are very wrong indeed. If that is so, then it is urgently necessary for us in Ireland, and our fellow European and world citizens, to cry halt and start inventing our way towards a new practice of peace. What is not an option is to let the war-machine continue as it is and hope that peace and development can fit into the cracks.

There are in fact very strong pointers to suggest that current defence thinking is flawed and in need of urgent replacement. Such pointers come by no means only from people whose experience lies outside the current military structure. They come, for example, from the Worldwide Consultative Association of Retired Generals and Admirals, which was founded in London in 1993. In 1996 it had 43 individual members, hailing from 24 different countries. Its moving spirit, the late Brigadier Michael Harbottle of the UK, described it as 'a military Pugwash', parallelling the organization of eminent scientists for peace:

> The Association's focus is on the prevention of armed conflict and the enhancement of stability and security through means other than military. It therefore acts in any situation or circumstance when peace and security are seen to be in danger or are already endangered. In consultation among its members, the Association will agree an opinion and make a proposal which can then be communicated to the respective Heads of State of the Association's members. (Harbottle, 1996)

These are people who have been at the brink during their careers and contemplated what lies beyond.

Heartfelt testimony was given recently by General Lee Butler, who before 1994 had responsibility for all US Air Force and Navy strategic nuclear forces. He told the US National Press Club of his decades-long adherence to nuclear deterrence and its associated beliefs.

> These are powerful beliefs. They cannot be lightly dismissed. Strong arguments can be made on their behalf. Throughout my professional military career, I shared them, I professed them and I put them into operational practice. And now it is my burden to declare with all of the conviction I can muster that in my judgement they served us extremely ill. (Butler, 1999, p. 7)

General Butler probes nuclear weapons strategy, concluding that the risks of nuclear war had never been rationally calculated. Such a strategy could have 'worked' only by negating its declared objective: the survival of the society employing it.

> I saw the arms race from the inside, watched as intercontinental ballistic missiles ushered in mutually assured destruction and multiple warhead missiles introduced genuine fear of a nuclear first strike. I participated in the elaboration of basing schemes that bordered on the comical and force levels that in retrospect defied reason . . . Sad to say, the cold war lives on in the minds of those who cannot let go the fears, the beliefs and the enmities born of the nuclear age. (ibid., p. 10).

The mindset against which General Butler is working here is thus not a thing of the past, nor a thing only of the United States. In 1995 the French Ambassador, defending underground testing in Mururoa, pointed out that:

> Nuclear deterrence is still a major strategic element of our two alliances [Western European Union and NATO] and the independent British and French forces are still

> contributing to this strategy. This was reaffirmed as recently as 1994 by the WEU Council at ministerial level. (*The Irish Times*, 19 September 1995)

He declared underground tests quite harmless; one trusts that France has also developed a technology for 'harmless' underground detonation of its weapons in actual war conditions.

A day or so later Ambassador Mouton reaffirmed his position in terms that should ring loud alarm bells as we encounter NATO/PfP and a common European 'defence' structure:

> The idea that nuclear deterrence is something that other countries reject is a completely wrong idea. It [is] the policy of all countries who are members of NATO and members of the Western European Union. It is the basis of our strategy. That should be remembered. *In this instance, if Ireland does not like it, they are isolated, it has to be said.* (*The Irish Times*, 21 September 1995; my emphasis.)

This contradicts Keatinge and Tonra's breezy assertion that such weapons are 'jealously guarded prerogatives of France and the United Kingdom' (op. cit., p. 12). We have also recently seen that the US in particular, in the 'War on Terrorism', is considering how nuclear weapons might be tactically employed (Rupert Cornwell, *Independent*, 12 March 2002; see p. 110 below). In any case, nuclear strategy, at the base of Western military thinking, challenges the entire edifice of international law with respect to war.

The World Court Project began as a movement to obtain an advisory opinion of the International Court of Justice – the UN's 'World Court' – on the legality of the threat or use of nuclear weapons. This initiative was endorsed by the UN General Assembly in December 1994. The five permanent members of the UN Security Council first opposed putting the question, then pressured the Court not to answer it. It was, thus, an historic act of independence by the World Court to reject this pressure and render its opinion on 8 July 1996. That judgment has not yet had its full impact, largely because it has been systematically misrepresented.

The Court decided that threat or use of nuclear weapons was indeed subject to international law (Chipp, 2001, p. 9). It found that, with one hypothetical exception, such threat or use would be illegal. The one hypothetical possibility concerned extreme self-defence, where nuclear weapons might be literally the only thing standing between a state and its destruction as a state.

The Court did not rule the threat or use of nuclear weapons legal *even in such a situation*; it said it could not at that time determine this part of the question. The judgment has since been presented as a failure on the Court's part to rule threat or use illegal. This is quite false: they have been ruled illegal, certainly in all but the hypothetical extreme and quite possibly in that extreme also. The Court President, Judge Mohammed Bedjaoui, made this clear:

> I cannot insist strongly enough that the inability of the Court to go further . . . cannot in any way be interpreted as itself evidence of a half-open door for the recognition of the legal permissibility of using nuclear weapons. (Chipp, 2001, p. 10; see also IICK, 2000, p. 183)

The Court unanimously added:

> There exists an obligation to pursue in good faith and bring to a conclusion negotiations leading to nuclear disarmament in all its aspects under strict and effective international control. (Farebrother, 2001, p. 6)

The neglect of this obligation means that at the heart of the 'defence thinking' of the major states of the EU and NATO there persists a black hole of utter contempt for international law on warfare. As we turn to the so-called 'conventional' arms trade, in which our fellow EU members are leading players, we might ask what precise convention renders these weapons 'conventional', and how we can repeal it.

The refinement of new weapons absorbs a huge proportion of our human ingenuity. Over one-fifth of the world's scientists are working on military-related research and development, more than half of these directly on weapons research. The world's investment in military research and development is of the order of $100 billion per year, exceeding expenditure on health care, new energy sources, education and other social needs (Regan, 1996, p. 200). War production is seen as central to future development and prosperity.

For example, in 1994 the arms industry employed one manufacturing worker in 10 in Britain, with an output representing one-fifth of the world arms market (Pilger, 1998, pp. 122–3). We thus treat 'progress' in new ways of killing one another as a central plank in building our home. Nowhere has generosity been so grotesquely parodied as in the solicitude of Western states for the 'needs' of other governments, whatever about their peoples. This eagerness has caused many a tragi-comic irony:

> When French Jaguar warplanes destroyed a cache of French Exocet missiles in Kuwait last week it was, as the political weekly *Canard Enchaîné* remarked, good news for France's weapon manufacturers. First, they sold the Exocets to Kuwait, where they fell into Iraq's hands. Next, they sold the AS-30 missiles to the French air force, which were used to destroy the Exocets. (*Independent*, 28 January 1991)

The governments that preach restraint and disarmament compete for arms sales to regimes the leaders of which they subsequently – sometimes even simultaneously – denounce as dictators and violators of human rights. In the face of the illegal annexation of East Timor, Britain and other arms-exporters blithely supplied the Indonesian government with weapons clearly intended for the repression of East Timor. A British-made Hawk jet was reported doing a 'flyover' during the militia rampage in late August of 1999, yet the Indonesians remained on the invitation list for Britain's major arms show later that year.

> I recall a visit in 1985 to the Headquarters of the Arab League in Tunis when the Secretary General informed

an Oireachtas delegation that the Iran/Iraq conflict was being sustained by the supply of arms from member states of the European Union and that one member state in particular was supplying both sides with armaments. (O'Kennedy, 1999, p. 1)

The point is not to prove what is already amply proved, but to *draw the connections* between what we know about the arms trade and what we know about the rest of our lives. Western societies are doing far more to create and disseminate the causes of war than they are doing to promote development and make war less likely.

The famines in the Horn of Africa made a huge impact on world opinion in the 1980s, but we rarely connect them with the incessant Cold War manoeuvrings for which that region was a major setting. The catastrophe in Somalia in the early 1990s:

> reflected a particularly cruel twist. The crisis was one for which the international community bore direct responsibility. Somalia had been a key playing field of Cold War rivalries, supported first by Moscow and later by Washington. The result was an extraordinary surfeit of powerful weapons 'left over' in the country. (Bennis, 1994, p. 157)

There are also countless examples of the 'opportunity cost' of weapons. 20 MIG29 fighters bought by India took the place of education for 15 million girls who do not attend school at all, whereas 40 Mirage fighters bought by Pakistan took the place of safe water for 55 million, family planning for 20 million, essential medicines for 13 million or health care for 12 million children (Regan, 1996, p. 203). All that is without reckoning the opportunity-cost of those two countries' nuclear weapons, not to mention the devastating effects of the consequent fear on their overall way of life and the shockingly present danger of an actual nuclear conflict (see Roy, 1999).

The war-machine neglects children, but it also incorporates them. The UN Security Council has passed a resolution condemning the practice of involving children in warfare.

> Some 300,000 boys and girls under 18 years of age, most of them under 15 and some as young as 7, are serving as regular soldiers, guerrilla fighters or porters, cooks, sexual slaves, and even suicide commandos in some 30 countries in conflict. Over the last decade, wars have killed 2 million children, left 6 million maimed, created 1 million orphans and 12 million refugees. (*The Irish Times*, 27 August 1999)

Sadako Ogata, UN High Commissioner for Refugees, has observed: 'For many children today, thou shalt not kill is no longer the norm; it is not even a pious wish' (Shawcross, 2000, p. 343). This scandal has recently been highlighted by Trócaire's 2002 Lenten Campaign.

Archbishop Makhulu of Central Africa has spoken of:

> the devastating effects of an unrestrained flow of arms on countries in Africa. You have to pinch yourself in disbelief at the number of people on crutches as victims of landmines. Sustainable development becomes an impossible dream as scarce resources are used to buy weapons of destruction from the West, rather than to meet the desperate needs of the people. Infrastructure is damaged, education ruined, schools and hospitals destroyed, and agriculture completely disrupted with farming land out of action for years ahead. We must stem the flow of weapons which is at the root of all this suffering. (McLean)

The armaments industry has taken root in Ireland over the past decade. Partly this is due to the arrival of new firms involved in arms production, such as Raytheon in Derry and Data Device Corporation and Moog in Cork. These arrivals have been documented by Afri's publications, *Links* and *What Price Peace?*, dealing respectively with companies in the Republic and in Northern Ireland.

Many existing companies are in a grey area, with products that are capable of either civilian or military applications. Others indicate that the 'military standard' to which their products are tested happens to be the accepted industry standard, illustrating how arms production has become 'normalized' within wealthy modern economies. Is Ireland going to drift into acceptance of, and a rapidly deepening entanglement with, the 'normal' production of lethal weaponry?

It is clear that the EU's common military policy has already made Ireland subject to the kinds of political pressure for which the arms industry is so notorious. Promoting the French Cougar helicopter in a keenly contested tendering process, the French Defence Minister wrote to his Irish counterpart:

> Devising and implementing a Common European Security and Defence policy constitues for our countries a major objective which deserves to be pursued and reaffirmed without respite. (*Sunday Business Post*, 9 June 2002)

Not to confront this question would be to abandon a major plank of our foreign policy tradition, just when that tradition needs to be reclaimed rather than quietly disowned. The arms trade is, as ever, a topic on which we need to challenge our EU and other neighbours, as well as ourselves. Rationalizing European 'military procurement' is far from a simple question of reducing inefficient duplication; it is also a move towards aggressive competition with the US, China and Russia in sales throughout the world.

Either we believe, as Foreign Minister David Andrews tellingly observed during the East Timor crisis, that 'the arms industry has no morality' (*This Week*, RTÉ Radio 1, 12 September 1999) or we do not. If we believe it, we need to act on it. A minimum requirement is complete openness about the precise military dimension of production here, and about the end-use of resultant exports. A further step would be to insist that all of what is called the 'peace dividend' yield 'new industries created to provide socially useful products and services around the needs of the communities' (Afri, 1999b, p.4.)

Both studies point out how difficult this is, given the ability of the armaments industry to influence, even shape, state policies, and given how much, at least in economies such as the UK, employment now depends on it. This is balanced by a grasp of how bad an economic bargain the arms trade represents from the point of view of productivity, efficiency and, above all, the creation of employment. One 1990 report on the UK economy estimated that a 50 per cent cut in military spending by the year 2000 could have produced 520,000 extra jobs, 1.84 per cent extra GDP and increased investment of 4.27 per cent (cited in Afri, 1996, p. 14). There is also huge potential in the urgently necessary area of technology for environmental recovery (Afri, 1999b, p. 15). These issues have also been explored in Amnesty's report, *Ireland and the Arms Trade* (Amnesty, 2000).

Thinking the Unfashionable: from Offence to Defence

Our distorted language emerges strikingly in our uncritical acceptance of all military activities as 'defence'. US General Lee Butler is particularly well placed to question this; from 1991 to 1994 he would have been the direct recipient of the order to go to nuclear war. He rejects the mantra that the Cold War at least prevented a major conflict between the superpowers. 'No one can possibly be an apologist for Stalin', he says, yet 'it appears that the Soviet motivation may have been chiefly to create a cordon sanitaire as a defensive perimeter . . . [;]the United States abandoned the difficult intellectual work of trying to understand the motivations of this enemy in favor of a simple demonization of him' (Schell, 1998, p. 195).

General Butler sees the whole nuclear arsenal as ultimately a mindless projection of fear:

> How is it that we subscribed to a strategy that required near perfect understanding of an enemy from whom we were deeply alienated and largely isolated? . . . While we clung to the notion that nuclear war could be reliably deterred, Soviet leaders derived from their

> historical experience the conviction that such a war might be thrust upon them and if so, must not be lost... Deterrence was a dialogue of the blind with the deaf. In the final analysis it was largely a bargain we in the West made with ourselves. (Butler, 1999, p. 9)

This recalls something we teach any young person going to a job interview: the other person, not knowing us, will try to 'read' us and respond, at every level from body-language through to what we say. Human action is interaction based on imperfect knowledge; how we present ourselves is crucial to how the other person reacts.

Does it ever occur to us that our 'defence' is the other society's danger? It isn't merely like it, it doesn't just contribute to it – it *is* the threat against which the other side in turn will react. This is what produces grotesque tragedies such as the loss of so many men in the Russian submarine *Kursk*. They were, it seems, prepared to die to 'defend' themselves from us, whom they have never known and who now cannot recall their names or number.

The US researcher Randall Forsberg has looked into the process of 'threat inflation'. In her work she pointed out that the US based its budgets on the assumed need to fight two simultaneous regional wars, each with a power as strong as pre-1991 Iraq. She noted that the charge that this provision is excessive 'is grave . . . For this reason, it is essential to spell out the evidence in some detail.' She concluded that there was currently no country, hostile to the US, which was significantly like pre-1991 Iraq, and that it would take 5 to 10 years, or much more likely 10 to 15, for any such country to become so.

Forsberg pointed out that in any case the US was equipping itself with twice the forces needed to fight the two hypothetical simultaneous opponents, and linked this reluctance to scale down with concerns over a revitalized Russia.

> There is an untried way to increase security while reducing costs and taking the potential future Russian

> threat into account. This is to cooperate with Russia in negotiating new limits and reductions in armaments, while at the same time strengthening the foundation for a more effective collective security system under UN auspices. (Forsberg)

She specified the complex of arms-control negotiations that could avail of this window of opportunity, and emphasized the *interactive* nature of such a strategic choice. Threat inflation would mean crucial human priorities forgone, but would also set US military budgets on a new rising curve 'as the forces of potential opponents grow and a new generation of weapon systems comes on line'. This was well before the recent huge budget expansion after 11 September 2001.

Andrew McLean points out that military defence itself causes insecurity, and J. David Singer of the University of Michigan has reminded us of how little actual security has been purchased by nation states since 1816 through their acquisition of the means of punishment. Singer calls for scientific research into different kinds of non-violent resistance and their precise effects, and retired Brigadier General Edward B. Atkeson of the US Army has called for similar 'nitty-gritty' analysis of notions such as 'citizen-based defence'. This analysis, he says, could significantly contribute to the development of strategic doctrine.

There is thus a wealth of analysis and reflection on a variety of crosscutting topics: non-offensive or defensive *versus* offensive defence; citizen-based *versus* army-based defence, and non-violent *versus* violent defence (see Moeller). Just imagine the difference that would be made if the price of even one Stealth bomber were diverted to systematic study of these topics every year! The Oxford Research Group has recently produced *War Prevention Works*, a study of 50 success stories of non-violent conflict prevention or resolution, sometimes in the midst of raging violence. Why is there no mention of these questions, and no discussion of what 'defence' means as such, in the one and only White Paper this state has ever produced on the topic (Ireland, 2000)?

Democratizing Democracy

> Democracy, peace and security are never givens. As we know, they must be redefined, recreated and re-secured in each generation. (Gerson, 2002a, p. 6)

A central question of the twentieth century was the fate of democracy. The Soviet threat after 1917 was soon counterposed by the menace of fascism; when that was defeated there remained the challenge of decolonization. Always there endured the rivalry between the West and the Stalinist systems, until the collapse of the USSR at the end of the Cold War in about 1990. Until then, the label 'capitalist' seemed to concede ground to the communist alternative, so a great deal of energy went into promoting less contentious substitutes such as 'industrial', 'affluent', and just plain 'modern'.

Now, however, with the USSR defeated and the Stalinist tyranny disbanded, we discover that the struggle had indeed been for and against capitalism. Yet there was strangely little triumphalism. Capitalism had apparently won because, in Margaret Thatcher's notorious words, 'there is no alternative'. Winning the Cold War meant little more than an adult winning a tug-of-war with a toddler. The triumph was less a political victory than a timeless scientific discovery: *that*'s what human nature has turned out to be!

History had arrived at Western liberal market society and the great social questions were no longer relevant. The new focus was on the people and practices that went with the free market: 'civil society' became the mantra not only for the former Soviet bloc, but also for societies elsewhere seeking to emulate our freedom and success. Yet the re-emergence of political issues in the richer societies has prompted a sense that, if a vibrant civil society is the cure for modern ills, we in the West are at least not suffering an overdose.

At home, we have tribunal evidence of the webs of influence associated with, for example, planning and the property market.

We have the scandalous failure of our health system to take adequate care of haemophiliacs and others whose lives have been devastated by contaminated blood products. Still worse has been the failure in turn to acknowledge this failure, to admit responsibility and attempt some genuine compensation. We also have seen the emergence of other grave problems such as sexual abuse.

Our concern here is not with these particular controversies – dreadful though they be – but with the evidence they offer that all is not well in the state of Ireland. Nor, for that matter, are things all that rosy in the state of Denmark, or indeed in any of the 15 EU member states, separately or together. The dismissal of the entire Commission in 1999 symbolized a complex of dissatisfactions, brewing at least since the run-up to Maastricht in the early 1990s. These, at times, seemed to concern relatively minor items, like travel expenses, secretarial appointments and the like, but overall there has been deep dissatisfaction with structures and accountability.

Professor Anthony Giddens observed in his concluding 1999 Reith Lecture:

> The European Union isn't itself particularly democratic. It has famously been said of the EU that if it applied to join itself, it wouldn't get in. The EU doesn't meet the democratic criteria it demands of its members. (Giddens, 1999)

There is a need, as Professor Giddens puts it, to 'democratize democracy'. The fact that governments are elected by popular vote – whilst hugely important and necessary – is insufficient to guarantee adequate airing of issues and implementation of policies in everyday life. It is like the point preachers often make: there is little sense in celebrating profound values for one hour a week, if the rest of our life is radically at odds with those values.

The many facets of what the Eurocrats label the 'democratic deficit' display one common feature: *silence*. Spin-doctoring and the like achieve a situation where people are deprived of information about problems affecting them or are prevented from effectively making an issue of them. The leaders who bewail the apathy of the citizen seem unaware of the cynicism of their own manipulations, which appear so often to seek the silence, rather than the reasoned response, of the public.

Though we lack the space to tease out all the challenges currently facing Western democracy, it is important to our subject at least to mention them, for two reasons. Firstly, we have already noted the paradox that we seem to apply our democratic system less to war than to any other topic; this is aggravated by the defects of that democracy as such. The consequences of this will be looked at below.

Secondly, we have the latest fashion, the 'Third Way' favoured by Tony Blair and many other European leaders, who also co-opted Bill Clinton. This builds on the Reagan/Thatcher legacy, which created an almost clear field for market forces, but claims to modulate it through more inclusive, 'big-tent' policies. This feature of Mr Blair's thinking feeds the tendency towards control-freakery and spin-doctoring, for which he is coming under mounting criticism.

The old, big questions have in fact refused to go away, even if they re-emerge in a novel guise. A case in point here is the Irish Pharmaceutical Union's opposition to government deregulation plans. Something is clearly afoot when the IPU invokes counter-globalization, confident it will strike a chord with the public:

> Irish pharmacies – particularly those in towns and suburban areas – will become more vulnerable to closure and/or takeover by profit-driven multinational conglomerates. (IPU, 2000)

Those ordinary citizens who invested in the privatization of Telecom Eireann have realized their impotence to hold anybody to account for their huge losses. We have endured anguish over, for example, teachers' pay claims and industrial action, to the point where there is scepticism about future national 'social partnership' agreements. Despite the Celtic Tiger, we have managed to increase economic inequality (see *The Irish Times*, 17 April 2002).

Here and elsewhere the new rhetoric of 'governance' is under strain. Anthony Giddens acutely poses the question:

> How can democracy and active government be sustained when they seem to have lost their purchase on events? .... A deepening of democracy is required, because the old mechanisms of government don't work in a society where citizens live in the same information environment as those in power over them. (Giddens, 1999)

Citizens are realizing that choosing wisely for a quiescent population is not just a task that leaders cannot be trusted to fulfil: it is in itself unfeasible. The issues involved, the information flows and practical tangles, emerge into actual experience and undermine our structured silence; the BSE case, the controversy over GM food and the Chernobyl catastrophe are graphic examples of this. The foot-and-mouth crisis of 2001 is a particularly telling challenge to consumerist politics and expert governance.

Professor Giddens's response to these challenges has been however to intensify, rather than to reconsider, his support for the Blair Which? Project (Giddens, 2002). He would probably claim merely to be recognizing the facts of the modern world, the famous 'bottom line': Tony Blair outdoes all others in branding his politics as 'modern', rather than Old Left, on the basis that they are grounded in the realities of market society. This extends also to the international scene, where Mr Blair is a leading exponent of globalization.

Where Margaret Thatcher fatuously declared there is 'no such thing as society', Blair and his supporters concede that it's probably okay for there to be a society – so long as it's civil! The 'Third Way' champions its protégé like an abusive parent: 'the people' can be 'cool', 'vibrant', 'proactive' and all the other good 'new' things, so long as they stay 'on message' and don't question the priority of business and the 'free market' on a local or global scale.

Like all abusive relationships, that between the spin-doctors and civil society arises from denial of a troubled history. Blair and his associates, and those other élites, including our own, who have been influenced by them, try to fillet our history and social structure to serve up 'Civil Society *à la mode*', but neither historical time nor social space favours them. We cannot employ the notion of civil society without evoking the underlying tensions of the social order from which it emerges.

Mr Blair's ally, Chancellor Schroeder, has recently taken court action to refute the allegation that he dyes his hair – particularly galling to someone so long devoted to bleaching his politics. To its critics, the Third Way has built its success on evading rather than tackling the problems of society. They point to the fact that, both in the West and globally, basic economic inequality not only endures, but has grown in recent decades. They argue that, though we have much to learn about resolving them, the persistent big questions will more and more bedevil the 'new politics', the more the 'new politics' tries to suppress them (see Barratt Brown, 2000).

This illustrates the futility of trying to democratize politics without democratizing society. I have argued that the travails of contemporary democracy are directly relevant to our topic of peace and war; the specific aspects of the Third Way that we have just discussed may have a further, more complex, relevance. One of the disquieting features of the past decade has been the ease with which our cosmopolitan élites have moved from the smoothest 'big-tent' rhetoric at home to the crudest, most inarticulate, campaigns of destruction abroad.

This does not mean that earlier governments, like Thatcher's or Reagan's, were intrinsically less bellicose; perhaps they simply lacked a particular skill in self-deception. What is most disturbing is how easily a leader like Mr Blair, priding himself on the morality of his domestic programmes and on his ethical foreign policy, can 'spin' virtually any action, such as the destruction of the lives of thousands of non-combatant Iraqis in the name of peace and security, as not only acceptable but morally obligatory (see Halliday and von Sponeck, 2001).

This in turn meshes with the fact, already discussed, that, in any case, the nearer we get to killing people the more secretive we allow others to become in our name. These two tendencies together yield a spiralling democratic deficit, as dangerous as it is difficult to grasp. Our most vital, and lethal, interactions with our fellow human beings are cocooned in a silence encased in turn in a protective shell of rhetorical democracy.

The same high-minded leaders who silence democracy at home in the name of the free market can, it seems, unblinkingly bomb 'lesser states without the Peace' and in each case invoke that question-stopper, 'the bottom line'. In each case – at home and abroad – there is a suspicious overlap of the political and the corporate 'bottom lines'; in each case also, silence is the currency. The challenge of breaking this silence, of rebuilding peace through democratizing democracy, is central to the recently launched European Network for Peace and Human Rights:

> We recognise the growing movements of protest throughout the world, many of them represented at our founding convention – peace workers, anti-nuclear and anti-militarist activists, environmental campaigners, religious groups, women's movements, labour movements, relief agencies, fair traders, indigenous peoples' organisations, human rights and other political organisations, including all those who have joined in protest at the corporate globalisation of trade, services, culture and the resurgent military-industrial complex. (ENPHR, 2002, p. 17)

Here civil society claims its own time and space, refusing the restrictions and repressive tolerance of the élites that seek to harness it. The ENHPR conference was electronically linked to the simultaneous Porto Alegre World Social Forum in Brazil. The common ground between workers for peace and globalization activists is well stated in the declaration of the 4th Assembly of the People's United Nations at Perugia in October 2001:

> We build in this way a global civil society increasingly visible and active, key player for a globalisation from below which can diffuse rights, democracy and justice, opposed to the neo-liberal globalisation imposed in these years by the economic power of the richest countries ... [These policies] imposed by supranational economic institutions, by the governments of rich countries and by multinational corporations have increased the profits of the few and the impoverishment of the many, increasing the inequality between the countries of the North and of the South of the world as well as within nations ... Reversing these trends is essential. Globalisation of the economy without globalisation of democracy will end up eroding even the small spaces of freedom and self-determination which exist today. What we want is the globalisation of human rights, of democratic processes, of the action of civil society: a *globalisation from below.*
> (Perugia Final Document, 2001, pp.1, 6, 10).

Irish Foreign Policy: the European Context

Obligations to our European Friends

It is often argued that, simply because we are EU members, or else because that membership has brought benefits, we ought not to stand aside from evolving military arrangements, whether direct or via NATO. Yet almost all would agree that the present EU is very far from a satisfactorily democratic polity. It would be very unwise now to pursue further military integration, given the unsatisfactory condition of European democracy even in far less vital areas of policy.

I say this as someone who welcomes the challenge of Ireland's addressing these issues. We need clarity about this benefits argument, however. If it means that we build up solidarity with our neighbours, and wish to maintain for all concerned what has proved worthwhile, well and good. It cannot mean that we should be prepared to perform morally repugnant actions just because we have received and/or hope to receive advantages; prostitution is prostitution, wherever it is carried out. We have indeed a responsibility to promote and protect our neighbours' welfare, as well as our own. But that cannot make right an action which would otherwise be wrong.

The question then is just what do we owe our associates. Surely our deepest responsibility to them is to build a way of life of which we can all be proud? If my friend is involved in a fight, I have a right, perhaps also a duty, to protect her or him. This does not create a right or a duty to attack the other party as such. Nor have we a right or duty to undertake beforehand to engage, on our friend's side, in whatever row he or she might choose or happen to embark on in the future.

This is all the more so if we know that our friend has, for example, an addiction, and/or a tendency to be quarrelsome and bear grudges. Not only do I owe it to some third party not lightly to threaten them on my friend's behalf – I also owe it to my friend. As Joseph Gerson of the American Friends Service Committee put it to the launch conference of the ENPHR in early 2002:

> In the United States, we have a saying 'Friends don't let friends drive drunk.' (Gerson, 2002b, p. 6)

Ireland, Europe and the Wider World

Whilst accepting the need to discuss security and defence with our EU partners, I am concerned how we approach such a discussion. My concern relates to two main questions: how we see Europe in relation to the wider world, and how we in Ireland see ourselves in relation to both.

How does the most recent statement of fundamental Irish perspectives, the 1996 White Paper on foreign policy, deal with these issues? It has much of interest to say about the needs of Europe and the world, but a vital link is left out of its argument. If we look at its list of challenges for the EU, we find that they consist of: social development around the Single European Market project; policy responses and 'transparency'; enlargement to include the other European democracies; ever-closer union among the whole EU population, and equipping the EU:

> to play a role commensurate with its responsibilities on the European continent and in the wider family of nations in pursuit of its essential interests and in the furtherance of its most fundamental values. (Ireland, 1996, p. 9 and Chapter 3)

Later on we find reference to 'the just needs of the developing countries' and 'a new and more equitable relationship between developed and developing countries' (ibid., p. 20, and 5.57-5.58). We are also told that 'much of the positive work of development is completely negated by armed conflict and the extensive availability of arms'(ibid., p.31, and 9.15-9.20).

This doubly fails to draw the vital links. We have a lack of integration between the statement of the position and interest of a Western country – in this case, Ireland – and the, apparently unrelated, needs and problems of the Majority World. We also have the specific phenomenon of war and its impact tacked on, as though merely related contingently to how 'we' in the West have defined and pursued our interests. Not only is this disquieting as it stands; the whole problematic is raised to a new pitch in the post-11 September context, as in the EU's latest self-description:

> Now that the Cold War is over and we are living in a globalised, yet also highly fragmented world, Europe needs to shoulder its responsibilities in the governance of globalisation. *The role it has to play is that of a power resolutely doing battle against all violence, all terror and all fanaticism, but which also does not turn a blind eye to the world's heartrending injustices. In short, a power wanting to change the course of world affairs in such a way as to benefit not just the rich countries but also the poorest.* (EU, 2001, p.78; my emphasis.)

It is not only the poor we shall always have with us – we are also assured an ample supply of poor analysis and bombastic rhetoric to accommodate 'them'. The plausibility, let alone desirability, of 'a power resolutely doing battle against all violence' may be left for the moment in the limbo of the absurd.

There is no reflection here on how Europe's pursuit of its interests and values has produced or accompanied a general injustice towards, and a specific tolerance and promotion of war within and against, the would-be developing countries. Once again, crucially, the *connections* are not made. If we do not make those connections and draw lessons from them, the best we can hope for is what Paul Rogers and Malcolm Dando have called a 'violent peace'. As Europeans, we have a responsibility, and the resources, to avoid this.

Some would see Europe as having laid the path which other regions have been more or less successful in following. Others would read the last 500 years as an appalling account of plunder, racism, and pollution, spearheaded by a Europe more aggressive and effectively expansionist than any imperium ever seen before. The truth may well lie between these two extremes. What is clear is that the debit side of Europe's activities over the half-millennium is heavy and written largely in blood.

I am not advocating an orgy of guilt. It is never useful – it is indeed a waste of energy – to assign a monopoly of evil to oneself or anyone else; there may well have been worse projects, with worse effects, in human history. *Our* history, however, concerns me here, and it involves chapters of wrongs: the take-off of European growth, fuelled crucially by the triangular trade in African slaves and West Indian sugar; the rapacious competitive colonization of the 'New World'; the trading, 'aid' and debt arrangements which have hampered the rise of decent, prosperous, viable democratic societies throughout the non-Western world; and the environmental degradation related to the extraction of timber, minerals and other raw materials for European industries.

This is, of course, far from the whole picture. Europe's legacy in philosophy, art, political ideas, science and many other areas is unique and a human treasure. I am very proud to be a European, raised with German as well as English as childhood languages. But every European must approach today's world with tact and restraint. The societies that bore us have been massively destructive, and imperious on a world scale. My father used to quote a saying: 'Those who would return with the wealth of the Indies, must set sail with the wealth of the Indies'. Whatever Europe was seeking abroad in its huge expansion, it certainly did not set sail with a peaceful and convivial self-confidence.

We need some self-searching about our relation to the wider world, and we have a treasure house of resources for the task. Our societies are fabulously wealthy, putting us in a position to take breathtaking leaps in reinventing ourselves and re-imagining our global position. Why could Europe not, even now, celebrate the millennium by declaring comprehensive peace on the world?

The US and World Security

Since I wrote the earlier version of *Defending Peace*, in 1999, much has happened, particularly the atrocities of 11 September in the US, and the resultant mobilization of the 'War on Terrorism'. The attention of most of the world has become focused, even as never before, on the US and its actions. In Ireland, perhaps more than elsewhere, those who have questioned the US response to 11 September have been met with the charge of being, for whatever reasons, anti-American.

That charge was linked to our specific topic by Niall O'Dowd, founding publisher of the *Irish Voice*, in an article in *The Irish Times* of 19 December 2001. I reprint here, word for word, the section of my 1999 essay on the US and our responses to it, written when none of us had remotely imagined the events of last year. Then I will attempt to bring the argument up to date in the even more troubled context of 11 September, and answer Niall O'Dowd's and similar charges.

Before 11 September 2001

I have debated long over having this section in my argument at all. In a word, I was afraid of being written off as 'anti-American'. The very presence of such a fear is in itself instructive. Few societies can ever have bulked as large in the minds of so many citizens of so many other contemporary societies as does the US in our world. Although its prominence was in many ways already well established, it was definitively proved by the US role in the Second World War. Its economic, logistical and political strength was awesome, as also the role it played in shaping the immediate post-war world at the global and regional levels. It is a society which I enjoy visiting, and which with many others I admire for its spirit, its dynamism, its creativity and its sense of enjoyment of life. It is also, however, a society with great unresolved problems in areas central to our present topic.

Whilst the impulse that guided some of its original white settlers was the push of European oppression and the pull of liberty, these were far from the only motivations in the building of the 'New World'. Its impact on the existing indigenous peoples, in both North and South America, was overwhelmingly destructive. Apart from accidentally imported diseases, deliberately imported arms contributed greatly and terribly to the destruction of whole peoples and cultures, a process whose nature and significance have not yet been acknowledged by or absorbed into contemporary US culture.

The gun, and the right of each individual to carry it as a symbol of liberty, have remained disturbingly central in the imagery, politics and economy of the contemporary USA, with predictably appalling, and apparently never foreseen, consequences. Its democratic political system has not prevented the enormous growth and concentration of corporate power, which it often seems to reflect rather than even attempt to control. That same system has also recently demonstrated its lack of entire maturity both in the topics on which it focuses and in the manner in which they are resolved.

I am not arguing here that we should be 'anti-American' in our attitudes. I am suggesting that we should be aware, and indeed wary, of any society as enormously influential as the US undoubtedly is, and work hard neither to be dazzled by the sunshine of its smile nor chilled by the clouds of its anger, whether real or imagined. This point is focused tellingly by the government's use, in favour of its argument for NATO's 'Partnership for Peace', of the most potent of all Irish-American symbols. The Explanatory Guide mentions President Kennedy, and his 'visionary speech to Dáil Eireann' in June 1963 (Ireland, 1999a), p. 10).

Far from being 'anti-American', I was a hero-worshipping 17-year-old standing on Clare St. in Dublin that day. All I saw of my hero as his motorcade swept around to Leinster Lawn was, with grotesque irony, the back of his head just as an assassin was to see it between hair-triggers five months later. I was so moved by his death that I wrote, and sent to a family friend who knew him, the following poem:

> Did fate not stay her hand
> In awe at what she planned?
> Did horror not cry out
> In anguish, at the rout
> Of that which beauty took a life to make
> And murder just five seconds took to break?

Not great poetry, maybe, but a great intensity of feeling and a fascination which endures to this day. The Kennedy legacy is still highly controversial. I will not even embark on that controversy here, save to note that I am still a 'sucker' for anything to do with the legend. All the revelations about his domestic political entanglements and his foreign policy machinations are still set, for me, in contradiction with his amazing brilliance of personality.

Yet that contradiction is very real, and we are left with its consequences. The Explanatory Guide to NATO/PfP quotes from President Kennedy's speech, finishing with the declaration that:

> no nation, large or small, can be indifferent to the fate of others, near or far. Modern economics, weaponry

and communications have made us realize more than ever that we are one human family and this planet is our home. (Ireland, 1999a, p. 11)

Like it or not, we must face the fact that as he spoke those words his foreign policy was actively engaged in taking over the former French role in Indochina, particularly Vietnam, leading to the destabilization of political structures in the south and the downfall – whether or not the assassination – of President Diem. It may well be that he would have proved more adept than Lyndon Johnson at reading the signs of US failure and disengaging; history was not to reveal that to us.

What is however clear is that, while the outgoing President Eisenhower, former supreme commander in the Second World War, warned of the 'Military Industrial Complex' in his farewell address, the New Frontier was embarking on a stunningly ambitious role of world leadership as proclaimed in Kennedy's Inaugural. It is also clear that the failure in Vietnam was a profound setback to these aspirations. The deep and unresolved damage of that wound is still with us, as was evident with Ronald Reagan's imagery of 'America walking tall', and the rhetoric about Operation Desert Storm as having finally laid to rest 'the ghost of Vietnam'.

There will be those who see all this as simply different ideological guises for US-led capitalist imperialism. Others may take the slightly more benign view of the US as 'the impulsive (if well-meaning) sole superpower' (Chesterman and Byers, 1999, p. 30). One way or another, there are the gravest reasons for doubting that US foreign policy is a consistent beneficent agency on the world stage. Old-fashioned anti-American propaganda? Hardly, if we are to heed for example the recent words of George Kennan, architect of 'Cold War containment', who was US Ambassador to Moscow in the 1950s and to Belgrade in the 1960s.

> [W]hat we ought to do at this point is to try to cut ourselves down to size in the dreams and aspirations we

direct to our possibilities for world leadership. We are not, really, all that great. We have serious problems within our society these days; and it sometimes seems to me that the best help we could give to others is to allow them to observe that we are now confronting those problems with a bit more imagination, courage, and resolve than has been apparent in the recent past.....[;] we must expect, I suppose, to appear to many abroad, despite our military superiority, as the world's intellectual and spiritual dunce, until we can change the image of ourselves we purvey to others. (Kennan, 1999, p. 6)

After 11 September

My aim in this section, now as in 1999, has been to convey some concerns about US policy. Rather than staking out a personal stance as an expert on, or critic of, the United States, I have listened to voices from within that society itself which to me carry the ring of truth. John Hume once pithily observed that on certain matters there is not much point in speaking to one's friends, when it is one's opponents who need to be addressed. There are also times when the converse is true: our real challenge is to speak meaningfully, courageously and effectively to our friends and, in a sense, to ourselves.

I hope that this will be received as a respectful indication, to citizens of the US, of what seem to me to be some of their own wiser counsels, rather than a generous helping of mine. I attempt this by responding to someone people both in Ireland and in the US can see as 'one of our own': Niall O'Dowd, founding publisher of *The Irish Voice* in New York. Mr O'Dowd has played a key role in our peace process and has been a source of clarification between Ireland and the US in so doing. It was therefore significant when, in late 2001, he published an article under the title 'Stuck in Neutral: Ireland's Smug America-Bashers' (*The Irish Times,* 19 December 2001).

Answering this indictment is perhaps a useful way of furthering our reflections on the US and the world after 11 September

2001. The events of that day were a massive criminal outrage, an 'unspeakable attack on the United States' as US Congresswoman Barbara Lee said on 14 September. Unequivocally, they should not have happened. Mr O'Dowd says in his article that those in Ireland who – like Congresswoman Lee in the US – question the US Government's response to these outrages reveal 'a certain mindset . . . which professes a bogus moral superiority when it comes to the use of force.' When one side in such an argument accuses the other of claiming moral superiority it raises the suspicion that the accuser knows there is a deep moral issue involved, but has not quite resolved it.

Mr O'Dowd's argument does not entirely dispel such a suspicion. He pours scorn on the suggestion that, if the US had used just ground troops, fewer Afghan civilians would have been killed. Mr O'Dowd dismisses this with the crude sneer, 'war by the Marquis of Queensbury rules', whose niceties, he tells us, do not apply here. His reason is the appalling nature of bin Laden and his associates, and indeed his assessment of Islamic fundamentalism in general. For the moment, we may note that he sees the threat as one before which civilian casualties are of, at best, diminished relevance.

Is this really his response to a whole century's attempt to minimize war casualties, particularly civilian ones? Is this where his coverage of the armed conflict in Ireland, and his close involvement in our evolving peace process, have brought him? Does his scorn apply to the findings of the Independent International Commission on Kosovo which, as we shall see below, raises serious questions about NATO tactics, including specifically the question of air strikes and civilian casualties, in Kosovo (IICK, 2000, pp. 5, 165, 177-184)?

Do they earn his condemnation for 'lack of nuance', in failing to perceive Kosovo as one of those US actions which 'are clearly correct and flow from a moral prerogative'? What exactly is this 'moral prerogative'? It seems much more like hot revenge than cool justice, and runs counter to the responses of many victims' relatives.

> On September 11, I lost my husband, Craig Scott Amundson, to the suicide attack that occurred at the Pentagon. Almost immediately, I had concerns about the United States' reaction to the attackers ... Despite any anger I had harbored, I knew that I did not want anyone anywhere to feel the deep sorrow I was left with ... I do not want my children to grow up thinking the reason so many people died following the September 11 attack was because of their father's death. (Amber Amundson, 2001, p. 2)
>
> Is this the path leading to peace, justice and the assurance of safety for American citizens in the years to come? Or is it a further contribution to the cycle of violence? (Ryan Amundson, 2001, p. 3).
>
> Other relatives added their voices. Judy Keane, whose husband Richard was killed, told CNN: 'Bombing Afghanistan is just going to create more widows, more homeless, fatherless children.' Jill Gartenberg, whose husband Jim was killed in the attacks, has told Fox News: 'We don't win by killing other people.' (*Observer*, 14 September 2001)

Where is the 'lack of nuance' in the letter to President Bush from Phyllis and Orlando Rodriguez, whose son Gregory was killed in the World Trade Center?

> Your response to the attack does not make us feel better about our son's death ... It makes us feel our government is using our son's memory as justification to cause suffering for other sons and parents in other lands. (ibid.)

Mr O'Dowd castigates our failure to see the difference between Kosovo and Afghanistan on one hand and, on the other, previous interventions in Vietnam and Central America, which 'are correctly scrutinised and criticised'. But yesterday's wars can easily be indicted, so long as today's are immune from current questioning. Today's war however is questioned, not only by Congresswoman Lee and by Craig Scott Amundson's widow and brother, but also for example by the relatives of Gregory Rodriguez and those of Abe Zelmanowitz, the hero praised by President Bush for staying to try to help his wheelchair-bound friend, at the cost of his own life (*Observer,* 14 September 2001).

Mr O'Dowd's broad-brush approach seems considerably less nuanced than the attitude of those, including victims' relatives, who have tried to turn the atrocities of 11 September, despite their dark intent and impact, towards the light.

> Rarely does the entire world come together as it did after September 11. This common bond of sorrow can bring about feelings of openness and cooperation as my family has found, but it takes a commitment to deal with your grief in a healthy way . . . I am horrified at the exploitation of these emotions to create an environment of fervent patriotism in which rational discussion is limited for the sake of political goals. Working to stop conditions which breed hate may be more complex and difficult than just dropping bombs, but the existence of evil does not have an easy solution. (Ryan Amundson, 2001, p. 3)

> 'I feel the American public has to join the international community in a meaningful way, and stop being an isolationist nation,' said Phyllis Rodriguez. ' . . . That's the first step: to learn about the sufferings and joys of other people. We have to find out why we are hated in other parts of the world.' (*Observer*, 14 September 2001.)

A reader of *The Irish Times* put his finger on one of the more bizarre of Mr O'Dowd's flights, which was to co-opt Martin Luther King, of all people, in his promotion of war as the answer. Mr Ciaran Feighery offered the following, from King's book *Strength to Love*, as a more appropriate summation of his philosophy:

> Returning hate for hate multiplies hate, adding deeper darkness to a night already devoid of stars. Darkness

cannot drive out darkness; only light can do that. Hate multiplies hate, violence multiplies violence, and toughness multiplies toughness in a descending spiral of destruction. The chain reaction of evil – hate begetting hate, wars producing more wars – must be broken, or we shall be plunged into the dark abyss of annihilation. (*The Irish Times*, 12 January 2002)

Martin Luther King, and the 11 September relatives I have quoted, pose a real political choice. We do not understand their stance if we assume that we can hear them, even honour them, and yet acquiesce in the current 'War on Terrorism'. They pose the radical question: whatever provocation we encounter, are we to respond out of the culture of violence or towards the culture of peace? Are we merely paying half-attention to a dead prophet and some unfortunate amateurs or do their voices make concrete the notions about peace and defence which we discussed earlier?

Mr O'Dowd would see them as misunderstanding the threat posed by al-Qa'ida and Islamic fundamentalism in general. That threat, for him, justifies the approach taken in the 'War on Terrorism' and the need to dispense with concerns about tactics and civilian casualties. Is he correct in his characterization of these people and movements in the first place and, if so, does this justify his approach to tactics and their consequences? We will return to these questions later, after considering a number of linked developments, including the crisis of the United Nations and the recent evolution of EU and Irish security policies.

The United Nations

It is widely believed the United Nations has failed, lacking the resources to intervene effectively in crises and stymied by the vetoes of the five permanent Security Council members. Both of these claims are in a sense true; both, however, are amenable to political debate and action by the member states. Until they are so addressed it will not be true that the UN has been tried and found wanting; rather, it will not have been tried at all.

The UN, of course, emerged from, and was shaped by, a particular conjuncture. Bringing together 50 or so nation states, it also embraced in its Charter the notion, 'We, the peoples', thus inscribing global unity and plural diversity at the heart of an envisioned new order. Its first priority was 'to save succeeding generations from the scourge of war'. This priority was seen as requiring a framework of law and social policy to make a more peaceful world.

The 'pessimist/realist' account tells us that the UN has had its successes and its failures, but that the latter are almost inevitable in a world of inequalities and conflicts. We are, it is said, unwise to ask more of the UN in such a world, because we risk overtaxing it and rendering it ineffective even in what it can hope to do. This story, told by the large powers which occupy centre stage in world politics, has gradually taken on the aura of received truth. That bespeaks the impact of those leading nation states, the jaded hopes of the other peoples of the world (and of many citizens of the leading nations too), and the use of rich nations' economic strength to ensure the quiescence of lesser states.

There is also an alternative story, which can be found for example in the book *Challenges to the United Nations – Building a Safer World*, published by the Catholic Institute for International Relations in 1994. The editor of that volume, the late Erskine Childers III, was the son of a President of Ireland who had made a unique contribution to 'taking the gun out of Irish politics' by his openhearted attitude to the political opponents whose colleagues had executed his own father in the Civil War.

His son in turn played a key part in setting an agenda to realize the dormant potentials of the UN Charter. This was recognized by his being one of the distinguished experts invited by the Department of Foreign Affairs to address its seminars prior to the publication of the 1996 White Paper. That day he spoke with a passionate eloquence and spelt out many truths.

> In our new world of instant global communication there is *no excuse* today for any major political and violent crisis to 'burst' upon us, already beyond conciliation, anywhere in the world; there is simply no such thing as an Iraq-Kuwait crisis or a Rwanda upheaval that is a real surprise. (Childers, 1995, p.5)

This clear and moving analysis was delivered in March 1995. Four years later, almost to the day, NATO launched its Kosovo bombardment.

The Framing of the United Nations

We realize today that a crucial aspect of power operates behind the scenes, setting the agenda for the overt and visible conduct of public life. To believe that power is always thus used is conspiracy theory; to deny that it is ever so used is equally self-deluding. The sensible position is an awareness that these things have happened and can happen, alerting us to whether they are happening when and where it really matters.

Power-mechanisms of these types have been operating on a world scale, in relation particularly to the UN. We cannot take any assertion about the UN at face value; we need always to ask who is making the statement, what interests are leading them, and how they are framing the UN in the light of those interests. We see this process of framing at work since the earliest years of the UN, for example in relation to the most basic questions about the world economy:

> Contrary to much ill-informed commentary, the UN was *not* poorly designed as only a peace and security organization ... The founders wrote into the Charter mandates to the UN to be the world leader in dynamic macro-economic and social policies to promote, and I quote, 'the economic and social advancement of all peoples.' The General Assembly was to adopt policies that would guide the specialized agencies ...
>
> In the event, a handful of industrialized powers have managed almost completely to disenfranchise the

> United Nations from the world economy, and to build up the IMF and the World Bank – which they effectively control – until these agencies are actually talked about as on a par with the UN. (Childers, 1995, p. 2)

Moreover, in dealing with the crises which are the consequences of this distortion, the UN, including the Security Council, has been marginalized, except when brought briefly on stage to legitimate actions undertaken by one or more powerful members.

Much, sometimes excessive, emphasis is placed on those sections of Chapter VII of the Charter which cover the authorization of military action in the last analysis. But even that Chapter calls for all possible diplomatic and other means, before force is used. Also, Chapter VI gives to the General Assembly the explicit role of considering 'any dispute, or any situation which might lead to international friction or give rise to a dispute' (Bennis, 1994, p. 155).

The use made of Chapter VII is highly dubious. There are authorities who argue that even the founding resolution for the Gulf War in 1991 – Resolution 678 – was invalid, because China abstained and the Charter requires all of the permanent members actively to concur. In any case, the use made of Resolution 687, passed at the end of the conflict, is deeply disturbing. Britain and the US carry out regular punitive air strikes on Iraq, over a decade later, in a context where they are, as former Under Secretary-General Sir Brian Urquhart puts it, becoming 'more and more isolated' (Urquhart, 1999a, p. 25).

Chapter VIII says that 'regional bodies' can play a role in dealing with possible conflicts before they reach full-blown crisis. We are often told that NATO plays such a role, in line with 'the current evolution of UN policy'. This story is extremely partial in every sense. NATO is at the same time the military alliance dominated by the richest industrial nations, who have excluded the UN from dealing with the basic structure and problems of the world economy (see Adams, 1994, p. 46.) These G7 countries include three of the five permanent members of the Security Council, who co-opt Russia to form the G8 when that suits, as in the final stages of NATO's intervention over Kosovo.

The key players here are those who have prevented the UN from making them accountable to the real international community. There is in fact a fully-fledged Chapter VIII regional arrangement in place, the Organization for Security and Co-operation in Europe, which evolved out of the Conference for Co-operation and Security in Europe, founded in 1973. Yet we hear a lot less of OSCE than we do of NATO.

NATO's attitude to the UN has been very complex and revealing. Sometimes it boasts of its UN mandate, for example in Bosnia. At other times it argues that the UN is powerless to bestow a mandate. When it so acts, it glosses over the legal niceties with the mantra, 'the UN increasingly relies on regional organizations these days'. Both the nature and the emergence of this 'reliance' will repay scrutiny.

NATO has set out to undermine both the OSCE and the UN over the last decade. In the NATO/PfP controversy our government tossed around quotations from the 1996 White Paper like snuff at a wake – appropriately enough! They did not quote the following passage:

> The Government believe that, as the only regional organisation to which all the states of Europe and North America adhere, the OSCE is uniquely placed to develop further its existing role as a focal point for European security cooperation ... We believe that the model should be based on the OSCE's comprehensive approach to European security. (Ireland, 1996, pp. 124, 125)

This perspective was being sidelined in the mid-1990s, and is now in danger of being overwhelmed, as with the withdrawal of OSCE observers in Kosovo on the eve of the NATO bombardment.

In addressing the current plight of the UN, we must realize that many difficult questions will arise. There is, for example, an important distinction between the scope of Erskine Childers's hopes for a fuller UN agenda and the more minimalist approach of, for example, Robert Skidelsky, who argues that:

> What we have in the UN Charter is a code of prudential rules designed to maximise the chances of peaceful coexistence – no more and no less. (Skidelsky, 1999, p. 8)

What is crucial for our present purposes, however, is the common ground between approaches such as Childers's and Skidelsky's, that in so far as anything approaching a real 'international community' exists, it exists, or needs to be built up, through the United Nations rather than NATO.

Dirty Work at the Crossroads: 'Desert Storm' to Kosovo

If the prevailing story is true, then an active central role for the UN is illusory. If it is false, the illusions lie in the monstrous untruths laid at its door. This is why Ireland's choices in the next few years are so crucial. We really cannot have it both ways, for those inviting us into their security parlour are the same demolition-gang who have been swiping at the prestige and efficacy of the UN now for more than a decade.

After the Berlin Wall fell, there was talk of a new dispensation, with Madeleine Albright speaking of 'assertive multilateralism'. Now, we are told, these hopes have perished, and we should not throw good peacekeeping after bad. What if the funeral is premature and the self-appointed chief mourners are furtively secreting an ether-soaked bandanna? If it can be shown that the chief powers in NATO have had a large part in shaping the alleged 'proven failure' of the UN, then we cannot take either their diagnosis or their prescription at face value.

In the lead-up to the Gulf War of 1991, the Security Council was in session on the subject of Iraq when it was informed that CNN was already showing the bombing of Baghdad. The Gulf War stands as a crucial point, where the UN (or rather the Security Council) was used precisely in the manner, and to the extent, chosen by the 'coalition'. Since that war, we have had several major crises. The conventional conclusion from all these is that the UN was weak or obstructive, and had finally to be set aside by the time it came to Kosovo.

There is ample evidence that each of these crises was manipulated by the leading NATO powers so as to use the UN as it suited them, most often as a scapegoat. This more than casts doubt on the current NATO-linked project for 'European security architecture'. That project is seriously flawed, grounded as it is in an alleged failure of the UN which was in fact a fabrication by the leaders of the project themselves. To suggest that this is indeed the case, we may look at some evidence on a few key points in the history of the past decade.

Somalia is cited as a prime instance of UN bungling, but the truth is more complex.

> On October 2, 1993, without the knowledge of the UN headquarters in Mogadishu, [US-led] Delta Force launched a helicopter-borne attack on a supposed [warlord] Aidid headquarters in Mogadishu, during which two helicopters were shot down and eighteen US Rangers killed. An estimated one thousand Somalis were also killed during this episode. (Urquhart, 1999b, p. 34; see also Bennis, 1994, p. 166)

Urquhart quotes *The Economist*: the US demanded a scapegoat, 'so finger the UN in general, and Mr Boutros-Ghali in particular' (ibid.). Chesterman and Byers note that 'the US troops had remained at all times under US command and control; it was legitimacy alone that the UN had given them.' (Chesterman and Byers, 1999, p. 29). The reaction to this débacle was to have appalling consequences in Rwanda in 1994.

> 'It has often been said that UNAMIR (UN Assistance Mission for Rwanda] was an operation which was created in the shadow of Somalia' (UN 1999b, p. 30).

When 10 of its troops were killed in Rwanda, Belgium withdrew from UNAMIR.

> A week later, on April 21, 1994, the UNAMIR Commander, Major General Dallaire, declared that with just five thousand well-equipped soldiers and a free hand to fight Hutu power, he could bring the genocide to a rapid halt. No military analyst whom I've heard of has ever questioned his judgment, and a great many have confirmed it. (Gourevitch, 1999, p. 150)

That day the Security Council voted to *reduce* UNAMIR by 90 per cent, influenced centrally by the US, though there was no question of US troop involvement. When eight African countries asked only for 50 armoured personnel carriers from Washington to aid their intervention, the US – then around $1 billion in arrears to the UN – demanded $15 million payment for them.

Gourevitch also spells out the machinations of the French, seeking to legitimize their support for the Hutu 'génocidaires'. They made a move the consequences of which we still suffer:

> the French government hit on the idea of billing a military expedition into Rwanda as a 'humanitarian' mission and carrying it out under the UN flag . . . [;] they embraced the Hutu Power military regime and its militias as the legitimate authorities of a state under rebel siege. (Gourevitch, 1999, pp. 155, 158)

Major General Paul Kagame, who had led the Tutsi resistance to the genocide, said he respected UNAMIR's leader General Dallaire, 'but not the helmet he wore' (ibid., p. 160), thereby articulating a key moment in the framing of 'the failure of the UN'.

In former Yugoslavia, the sole superpower is far from the sole culprit: much mischief dates from the competition among, particularly, the Germans and the Russians for client states to sponsor. Pre-emptive recognition of parts of Yugoslavia as independent states, before the consequences were thought through, encouraged the bloody dismemberment that occupied the 1990s.

A central charge in the case against the UN is the fate of UNPROFOR (UN Protection Force) in Bosnia. The UN was sidelined from the very start, Bennis tells us:

> The Conference on Security and Cooperation in Europe
> (CSCE)[now OSCE], the one potential agency with a
> European-wide mandate encompassing both West and
> East, as well as Russia, was kept out of the Yugo-loop,
> even during the historic CSCE summit in November
> 1990. (Bennis, 1994, p. 169)

UNPROFOR was set up, lightly armed and without a mandate to use force, against the advice of UN Secretary-General Boutros Boutros-Ghali. When he suggested a 70,000-strong NATO-led force to achieve humanitarian aims and safe areas, the US declared this unacceptable (Urquhart, 1999b, p. 33). The question of air strikes against the Serbs, arising directly from this refusal to risk troops on the ground, became the focus of a still-enduring denigration of Boutros-Ghali and the UN.

> In spite of Boutros-Ghali's installing a system by which
> the UN commanders on the ground, in cooperation with
> NATO commanders, would have the major voice in call-
> ing for air strikes, from now on he would be portrayed
> in Washington as the person who had blocked the US
> from using air power to end the war. (ibid.)

At the crucial stage in Srebrenica, the French General, Janvier, refused air strikes to support a contingent of 700 Dutch troops. The Dutch have since made some admission of their guilt in having stood by during the massacre. The French, in their own official inquiry, have excluded press and public from the questioning of General Janvier:

> [it is] essential to establish how Janvier was instructed
> by his political masters and what passed between him
> and [Serbian commander] Mladic in the three meetings
> in June 1995 . . .; there may be a good case for an indict-
> ment at the Hague. (Henry Porter, *Observer*, 22 April
> 2001)

Boutros-Ghali was totally misrepresented, being blamed for having had 'operational control' of US forces which he did not control, whilst his request for 35,000 more peacekeepers was rejected.

There is an old Jewish story to illustrate the meaning of 'chutzpah'. It concerns a young man who murders his parents and asks the court to have mercy on him as an orphan. This is the logic of the arguments about the UN lacking moral and practical authority: it has been systematically deprived of both throughout its lifetime, particularly since the end of the Cold War opened up a serious danger of it moving to centre-stage (see p. 77 below).

The UN: Last Best Hope or Ultimate Delusion?

We should, of course, expose the gap between the UN's aspirations and its achievements, but we should also expose just how that gap is created and maintained. Global democracy, even in an initial 'surface' version, will never be given as a gift, or recognized as a right, by the rich and powerful states, but must be demanded by the Majority World and those elsewhere who share or support their struggle.

> Global civil society renews its demands to governments and parliaments: . . . to stop the wars in progress and place the UN in the position of exercising its proper functions and powers, for implementing the UN resolutions on the rights of peoples, for preventing and ending conflicts, maintaining peace and reconstructing the areas destroyed by conflict, establishing an adequate world system of common security, avoiding that individual countries or individual alliances take over the role and functions of the UN, creating an international military police force as provided by article 43 of the Charter and maintaining the regional security systems under the control of the United Nations as set out in Chapter VIII of the Charter. (Perugia Final Document, 2001)

There is a striking contrast between the furtiveness and evasiveness of leading NATO members about events in Somalia,

Bosnia, Rwanda and elsewhere, and the UN's self-criticism of its past record and future challenges. This can hardly be overstated: in three major reports, dealing respectively with Bosnia, Rwanda and peacekeeping as such, the UN has subjected itself to a scrutiny utterly unimaginable on the part of our domestic political, or other, elites. It is also conducted in language, direct and 'unspun', which is a breath of fresh air.

The Carlsson Report on Rwanda straightforwardly criticizes UN Headquarters, including then head of Peacekeeping Operations, Kofi Annan, for failures in acquiring, assimilating and acting on intelligence at the inception of UNAMIR.

> The overriding failure to create a force with the [necessary] capacity, resources and mandate . . . had roots in the early planning of the mission . . . The responsibility for this oversight . . . lies with . . . in particular the Center for Human Rights and [the Department of Peacekeeping Operations].(UN,1999b, p. 22)

These sharp criticisms lend massive weight to the further conclusions:

> The Member States which exercised pressure upon the Secretariat to limit the proposed number of troops also bear part of the responsibility. Not least, the Security Council itself bears the responsibility for the hesitance to support new peacekeeping operations in the aftermath of Somalia. (ibid., p. 23)

Kofi Annan wrote the *Srebrenica Report* and spares neither himself nor the rest of the UN structure. He openly admits inexcusable faults and the failure to make adequate use, both deterrent and operational, of NATO air power:

> we did not use with full effectiveness this one instrument at our disposal to make the safe areas at least a little bit safer. (UN, 1999a, p. 107)

As with Carlsson, this candour adds weight to his analysis of the broader context.

> The international community as a whole must accept its share of responsibility for allowing this tragic course of events by its prolonged refusal to use force in the early stages of the war. This responsibility is shared by the Security Council, the Contact Group and other Governments which contributed to the delay in the use of force, as well as by the United Nations Secretariat and the mission in the field. (ibid., p.111)

Carlsson links its criticisms with the Secretary-General's observations:

> In his report, the Secretary-General encouraged Member States to engage in a process of reflection to clarify and to improve the capacity of the United Nations to respond to various forms of conflict. Among the issues highlighted, he mentioned the gulf between mandate and means and an institutional ideology of impartiality even when confronted with attempted genocide. As is clear from the above, both of those issues formed part of the key failings of the UN in Rwanda. The Inquiry believes that the process of analysis and discussion suggested in the Srebrenica report should be undertaken promptly in order to address the mistakes of peacekeeping at the end of this century and to meet the challenges of the next one. The Inquiry hopes that the present report will add impetus to such a process. (UN, 1999b, p. 38)

The independent panel on UN Peacekeeping produced the Brahimi Report in August 2000 on the generic problems and needs of UN peacekeeping. It summarizes many points we have already noted and surveys the UN's resource deficiencies, observing for example that:

> after over 50 years of deploying military observers to monitor ceasefire violations, [the UN] still does not have a standard database that could be provided to military observers in the field to document ceasefire violations and generate statistics. (UN, 2000, para. 221)

Regarding the most crucial resource, contributions of personnel from member states, the picture is very gloomy.

> In contrast to the long tradition of developed countries providing the bulk of the troops for United Nations peacekeeping operations during the Organization's first 50 years, in the last few years 77 per cent of the troops in formed military units deployed in United Nations peacekeeping operations, as of end-June 2000, were contributed by developing countries. (ibid., para. 103)

This generalizes the Carlsson findings:

> Recognition is due to those troop contributing countries, in particular Ghana and Tunisia, which allowed their troops to remain throughout the terrible weeks of the genocide, despite the withdrawal of other contingents. In sum, while criticisms can be levelled at the mistakes and limitations of UNAMIR's troops, one should not forget the responsibility of the great majority of United Nations Member States, which were not prepared to send any troops or matériel at all to Rwanda. (UN, 1999b, p. 32).

The Brahimi Report is specific on the causes of this problem, including the fact that:

> developed States tend not to see strategic national interests at stake. The downsizing of national military forces and the growth of European regional peacekeeping initiatives further depletes the pool of well trained and well-equipped military contingents from developed countries to serve in United Nations-led operations.
>
> Thus, the United Nations is facing a very serious dilemma . . . Even if the United Nations were to attempt to deploy a KFOR-type force [in e.g. Sierra Leone], it is not clear, given current standby arrangements, where the troops and equipment would come from. (UN, 2000, para's 105, 106; see pp. 110–111 and 128 below)

Two major crises erupted during this period of intense self-scrutiny, which, we shall see, in different ways put the UN, and member states' support for it, to the test: Kosovo and East Timor (see pp. 73–84 and 101–106 below).

Whatever happens, we need a forum for comprehensive conflict prevention and resolution that can respect and promote the rule of international law. If those who perceive this need have the courage to subvert the current shambolic 'consensus', that will launch a serious effort to make the UN the key player among, rather than the plaything of, the world's power brokers. Some people, because of long and bitter experience, will reject this notion. It would be disastrous for their justified anger and scepticism to lend plausibility to those who have created the problem and prevented its effective solution.

The answer to the current impasse of the Security Council is to change the law – in this case, the constitution, the Charter itself. Permanent membership and the power of veto could be expanded, reassigned, abolished or otherwise altered by the ultimate authority of the UN, the General Assembly.

Or could they?

> Article 108
> Amendments to the present Charter shall come into force for all Members of the United Nations when they have been adopted by a vote of two thirds of the members of the General Assembly and ratified in accordance with their respective constitutional processes by two thirds of the Members of the United Nations, *including all the permanent members of the security council.* (UN, 2001, p. 66; my emphasis.)

It would be very naïve to suggest that this situation can be resolved overnight without damaging the UN itself. It would be even more naïve to conclude that that should be the last word: to use the difficulties of reform as a pretext that it should not even be attempted.

For domestic politicians to say nothing can be done about industrial safety, public transport or white-collar crime because the law is incomplete on some such topic would elicit the response that we should change the law. The General Assembly is treated in practice in a manner which no democratic parliament would tolerate, with the key decisions on the UN's first priority – the scourge of war – effectively sealed off from its scrutiny and oversight.

We need to apply to international relations and global problems an understanding which has been slowly, painfully and as yet incompletely applied in domestic politics. This is that the most inclusive forum and decision process are the best, precisely because they bring to bear the widest and most enriching perspectives. Any argument that such a forum should be bypassed always raises the suspicion that something is happening, or being planned, which would not be allowed in open forum. Any restrictions on, or delegation from, the open working of such a forum must be exceptional, provisional, provided for by that forum itself for reasons decided by itself and, most important of all, instantly revocable by that forum itself.

Kofi Annan Interview and Editorial

While the Kosovo crisis was developing, and NATO's promotion of its 'Partnership for Peace' was in full swing, the UN Secretary-General visited Ireland. His interview with Mark Brennock was reported in the *The Irish Times* of 23 January 1999, which issue also had an editorial entitled 'The Partnership for Peace'. This interview was in many ways a crucial occasion, and it provides a focus for a great deal of my argument.

I have been arguing some of the following points:
- we are faced with a choice, a decision as to the future shape of Irish foreign and defence policy;
- rather than debating this choice in a clear and open way, we are in danger of its being made tacitly for us;
- those who are driving the decision for radical change to our policy present this change as almost inevitable, both morally and practically;

- they base this claim on a reading of the international scene, and particularly of the reality and potential of the UN vis-à-vis organisations such as NATO;
- this reading is a persuasive construction, far more than it is an objective recognition, of 'facts';
- the 'constraints' which allegedly dictate this course of action are not in fact stone walls, but doors and pathways, which its proponents have quite skilfully closed down to create the illusion of a single street where only one-way traffic is possible.

My own case also is a rhetorical one; I also am trying to draw the reader into the future I want to see. Where I hope that my approach differs is in that I want to insist that there is a wide range of possible futures: we are burdened with choosing and shaping the one we want, and cannot unload that burden onto the shoulders of leaders or the gravity of 'the bottom line'.

I want to look in some detail at the Kofi Annan interview, and the editorial, to unpick how the occasion is constructed and used to further the case for the inevitability of a certain kind of change. (In my analysis below, I indicate paragraphs from interview and editorial with the letters 'I' and 'E' respectively). Lest the point of my critique be misinterpreted, I must make it clear that all this is done on the basis of my enormous respect both for Mr Annan himself and for the office which he holds.

The editorial, the final product of the whole process, puts itself forward as drawing conclusions from what it says the UN Secretary-General says in the interview:

> As this State decides whether to deepen its involvement with security organisations in Europe, there is much it can learn from Mr. Annan's perspectives on contemporary peacekeeping. (E, 2)

This is after Mr Annan's credentials as a teacher have been put neatly in place:

> Mr. Annan is now well into his term of office and fully addressing the UN's political and structural problems. He has demonstrated great skill in tackling them, in defining the opportunities and limits of his own leadership role and asserting the independence which must underlie it. (E, 1-2)

Mr Annan, we are told, 'makes much of how the end of the Cold War has altered the nature of peacekeeping' (E, 3). Mr Annan may well have done so, but readers of the interview are not in a position to confirm this. Having spent a couple of paragraphs profiling Mr Annan and quoting his praise for Irish contributions to UN peacekeeping, the interview proceeds:

> The nature of UN peacekeeping, however, has changed in recent years, with major missions, such as Sfor (Stabilisation Force) in former Yugoslavia, being organised and commanded by NATO rather than the UN itself. With the UN now encouraging regional organisations such as NATO to organise UN-mandated peacekeeping operations within their own region, can Ireland continue its commitment to peacekeeping while having nothing to do with NATO? (I, 6)

This paragraph is very complex. The first sentence, which does indeed 'make much of' changes in UN operations, is an observation by the interviewer, not a quotation from the interviewee. It is nothing, however, to the question put before when we next hear from Mr Annan. Not only have we the heavily loaded notion of the UN 'encouraging' NATO's behaviour, rather than tolerating it or having it forced upon it; we then have the crucial question of how Ireland might relate to all this.

It appears simply to be raising the by now conventional issue of whether the world has so changed that it is appropriate for us to move closer to NATO. What it actually asks, though, is whether we will be left with any useful peacekeeping future at all if we do not! Mr Annan's response, diplomatically recognizing that Ireland would make its own decision, goes on to say that 'as far as the UN is concerned, there is no impediment' to our continued role in traditional peacekeeping if we were involved with NATO: 'We should continue to be able to work with you in the way we always have' (I, 8).

It is important to note that this is a simple statement that we could in fact continue to be involved in traditional operations, rather than an endorsement of NATO or of the new operations led by it. This matters, because of the treatment of the nature and legitimacy of these latter operations in the bulk of the interview, and in a couple of key sentences of the editorial. The latter informs us that:

> Neutrality between warring states has given way to impartiality in the execution of the mandates agreed by the Security Council. (E, 4)

This may very well be so – whatever precisely it means – but it is not an account of the reported views of Mr Annan; it is not even an observation by his interviewer. Never mind: pop it in, it will help things along. Mr Annan does, as reported, describe the new forms of intervention led by NATO and some other groupings. He points out that whilst directly UN-led operations now have far fewer troops than before, the total involved in peacekeeping remains more or less constant (I, 10). He goes on to argue that the UN will remain necessary for situations where regional bodies cannot operate outside their own areas, and observes:

> I think we shouldn't write off peacekeeping yet. When we look around this messy world we live in there is going to be a continuing need for their services. (I, 11)

Here we approach the crux. How can those services best be provided? Who should decide on them and who should run them? The interview has invoked the notion of 'UN-mandated peacekeeping operations'(I, 6) and the editorial has spoken of 'mandates agreed by the Security Council' (E, 4). The interviewer himself goes on to pose a major problem with these notions:

> The US and British decision to bomb Iraq recently without seeking explicit UN Security Council approval once again undermined the UN's desire to be seen as the arbiter of international disputes. The US decided to do what it wanted, and Mr. Annan, who himself brokered a deal to avoid air strikes last February, could only watch. (I, 15)

Mr Annan is asked whether the bombing of Iraq was then legitimate:

> [H]e answers carefully. 'You saw the reactions of certain Security Council members, including some of the permanent members, to that action. They made it clear that they did not consider it as something that the Council has sanctioned. The British and the Americans believe they had authority on the basis of existing resolutions to do this, so the best one can say is that there is a difference of interpretation. The Council is now trying to deal with the morning after and see where they go from here. Even though they are at the moment divided I hope that they will find common ground.' (I, 18 & 19)

The interviewer asks him to say whether Britain and the US were right to act:

> he laughs politely and declines. On whether NATO could take military action against Yugoslavia over Kosovo without a further UN Security Council vote, he also chooses his words carefully. (I, 20)

Mr Annan goes on to outline the difficulties in Kosovo, and the desirability of a negotiated political settlement. He is then asked whether there is an obligation on NATO to seek specific Security Council authorization before it takes military action.

> The Council as a practice has encouraged all organisations to refer to the Council on issues of this nature,' he says. Should this practice be continued in the case of possible military action against former Yugoslavia? He laughs politely again and says: 'I think I've given you enough there'. (I, 24)

It is deeply ironic that, while the spin-machines depict him and the UN as 'encouraging' NATO in its ambitions for leadership, he uses that very same verb as diplomatic code for the hope that such bodies might be persuaded to respect the UN in the first place. It is also clear beyond any doubt, from the very way in which the interview is reported, that the UN Secretary-General feels himself hugely restricted in what he can do and even in what he can say in this regard. So much for the opening depiction in the editorial, designed to represent him as not only willing, but enabled and permitted to address 'the UN's political and structural problems', and for the notion that he can actually exercise the 'independence' which quite clearly his role requires.

All this makes it particularly bizarre that the editorial can report him on this complex of issues by saying that 'Mr Annan cites the joint NATO/United Nations peacekeeping and peace building mission in Bosnia as a model' (E, 4). Nowhere in the interview as reported does he do this; the *interviewer* gives it as an *example* of the new type of operation, and the ambiguous word 'model' is not used in the interview at all, by either interviewer or interviewee.

This again is no small pernickety matter. The reference to models is followed by the runic observation that '[m]andate and legitimacy are intimately connected' (E, 4). Quite so, we would all agree, though not all of us would see Mr Annan as saying or implying that the connection is currently being honoured in the observance. All of this becomes more fascinating when we read the Department of Foreign Affairs Explanatory Guide to Ireland and NATO/PfP. This document refers to the Secretary-General's visit in January 1999, and gives a précis of the issues, just as we have seen them covered in the *Irish Times* interview. The précis ends thus:

> While noting that traditional observer missions may still suffice in certain situations, the UN Secretary General has specifically cited the joint NATO/UN peacekeeping and peace-building mission in Bosnia as a model of credibility and legitimacy. (Ireland, 1999a, pp. 6-7).

If this conclusion is drawn from *The Irish Times* of 23 January 1999 it is a distortion. If it is drawn from elsewhere we have good reasons for wondering through what tortuous process it has been generated. It should also make us extremely wary of any reassurance that Irish participation in NATO's PfP would be subject to the authority of the UN; the UN currently 'authorizes' what the great powers and the one superpower allow it to 'authorize'.

Letting Slip the Dogs of War

Our debate about Irish foreign policy is about a *process*: what is going on; where are we headed; is the process sound; do we need to alter it? We have grounds to be wary of the advice and promises of our political establishment, given their past performance.

Our Politicians and Neutrality

We are told regularly – with panicked frequency in the Nice debate – that opponents of the establishment line are dishonest. The issue of honesty clearly arises – but just who is telling the truth? The Explanatory Guide on NATO/PfP tells us that in the 1970s Ireland:

> joined the European Economic Community and accepted without reservation the process of European

> integration, *which was understood to include some common defence role in due course.* (Ireland, 1999a, p. 10; my emphasis.)

This is demonstrably false. Concerns about the military implications of EEC entry were so marked in 1972 that the then government explicitly told us, in the White Paper of *that* year:

> the Irish Government in applying for membership of the Communities, declared their acceptance of the Treaties of Rome and of Paris, the decisions taken in their implementation and the political objectives of the Treaties. The Government have, furthermore, declared their readiness to join as a member of the enlarged Communities in working with the other Member States towards the goal of political unification in Europe. *It should, however, be emphasised that the Treaties of Rome and Paris do not entail any military or defence commitments and no such commitments are involved in Ireland's acceptance of these Treaties.* (Quoted in Maguire and Noonan, 1992, p. 45; our emphasis.)

We are not being told the truth, overall or in detail.

Some leaders have rejected neutrality, believing we should become fully engaged in the new 'security architecture'. Others oppose that view, or flirt with opposition to it, for political advantage. The first group have been less than open about opposing neutrality in principle, and the second less than open about their readiness to abandon it in practice. We could label them the 'fully gung-ho' and 'faltering faithful' tendencies, or 'FG' and 'FF' for convenience.

Others have participated in an exercise directed by FF and FG: the whittling away of our distinctiveness in foreign and security policy. It resembles a hard cop/soft cop routine. FG implied that our non-membership of military alliances was somehow deplorable, a failure of moral courage and political maturity. FF slightly disagreed, but found neutrality embarrassing, a secret to be shared with electorates while in opposition, but not trotted out in front of the big boys in Brussels.

A central issue here is Ireland's stance during the Second World War. There was indeed some ambivalence in that stance, which was, of course, also supported by the opposition. There were also some whose hostility to Britain led them to support fascism – not to mention those right-wingers who required no lead because they were already there. The central issue however is whether Ireland, *before 1939*, should have become committed to a military alliance, ruling out any choice on our part when the crunch came over Poland. It would be astonishing if we had no concerns about what Ireland should have chosen then. We do nothing for those, or related, concerns if we let them hide from us the prior duty to have a real choice in the first place.

Ireland in the 1950s had, amongst other things, a sense of a political history different from that of Britain and similar nations, and had an affinity with the newly independent nations entering the UN in the 1950s and 1960s. This was articulated by Frank Aiken as Minister for External Affairs and expressed in policy positions, and UN peacekeeping activities, which said something about where Ireland stood. Few of us believed we were morally sovereign or superior; we were simply making sense of where our history had located us, and stating policies and priorities as we saw them.

This was no fully thought-out, uniquely virtuous position, but a product of circumstances and values, summarizing our past with a view to building one of a range of possible futures. It is easy for its opponents or its half-hearted supporters to fix on 'neutrality' as a word and bemoan its alleged 'incoherence'. All political principles are provisional statements, always needing conceptual refinement and improved implementation. We do not jettison concepts like 'justice' or 'equality' because we disagree about their meaning or fail in pursuing them. I will return to the contemporary implications of neutrality in the concluding section of this essay.

FF and FG have in common a mantra that (a) nothing currently envisaged will compromise our principles and (b) if any significant change were contemplated, it would be put to the electorate. These seeming reassurances in fact provide latitude for creeping change without reference to the electorate: those who are concerned have nothing now to worry about, and will be told to worry if and when the time comes!

SEA/Maastricht/Amsterdam: EU Military Policy Evolves

Dr Garret FitzGerald is one of our politicians who rejected neutrality and wanted a policy including military involvement. But now he tells us there was nothing there to reject: Irish neutrality is apparently a myth with no basis in historical reality (*The Irish Times*, 24 April 1999). One must wonder then why he said the following in 1987:

> the Government are committed to preserving Ireland's neutral position outside military alliances . . . [and] it would have been superfluous to include a declaration to that effect in the [Single European] Act. (CMRS, 1987, p. 7)

Why not just say the policy inquired about was as real as Santa Claus?

As for 'superfluous' treaty statements: if you have a fundamental policy position in negotiating a binding agreement, you spell it out. If not, it recedes to an alleged implication of what *is* spelt out; one cannot but wonder why. A highly plausible answer is given by looking at the text of the Single European Act. All but two EEC members – Denmark and Ireland – were in the Western European Union, where military matters were pursued. As Denmark was anyhow in NATO, Ireland was the only country for which a principle was at stake. Yet the Treaty never once mentions Ireland, or even spells out our general point of principle:

> Nothing in this Title shall impede closer co-operation in the field of security between certain of the High Contracting Parties within the framework of the

Western European Union or the Atlantic Alliance [i.e., NATO]. (SEA Article 30, 6(c), in Ireland, 1986, p. 62)

The government's explanatory guide to the SEA told us that the above wording was put in 'so as to take account of the fact that Ireland is not a member of a military alliance' (ibid., p. 28). Yet Ireland is not mentioned, and the alliances are.

It seems bizarre to spell out our policy to ourselves, but not burden our fellow EEC members with it. It bespeaks a perception of neutrality not as a myth but as a real stumbling block to the others' plans or to our acquiescence in them. So it proved in April 1987, as Mr Justice Henchy put it:

> Title III of the SEA is the threshold leading from what has hitherto been essentially an economic Community to what will now also be a political Community ... If Ireland was to ratify the treaty it would be bound in international law to engage actively in a programme which would trench progressively on Ireland's independence and sovereignty in the conduct of foreign affairs. (CMRS, 1987, p. 9)

Ratification had halted when, in late December 1986, the Supreme Court upheld Raymond Crotty's right to argue his case. The April ruling spelt out the problem facing the Government – no SEA without a referendum.

This profoundly embarrassed our political leaders vis-à-vis Brussels; Ireland was 'holding up Europe'. The government's solution proved a watershed. It could have decided that, as the Supreme Court had found problems with Title III (on foreign policy), that Title should be put to a referendum; no more was required. The decision, however, was to hold a referendum on the entire SEA, single market and all. It was calculated that the electorate would say yes to the whole package, including structural funds and the like, whereas they might well say no to the evolving common foreign policy considered on its own.

This misrepresented the Supreme Court's insistence on

foreign policy and security as the area requiring a referendum. We have never had a referendum on foreign and security policy as such. It was always run together with arguments over possible economic gains and losses. This refutes the argument that we owe it now to our EU neighbours to sign up to certain military arrangements: we would not have gone this far except for the threatened loss of benefits! Successive governments have spelt out neither an assertion nor an abandonment of neutrality and, when push came to shove, they muddied the waters.

On the SEA, Mr Haughey argued:

> The Taoiseach, Fine Gael and Labour ministers have misled the public, and misrepresented the Single European Act by claiming that military aspects of security are specifically or categorically excluded ... It is obvious that once this Act is ratified Ireland will be under acute pressure to go some further distance. (Dáil Debates, 9 December 1986)

Within months, back in government, he steered the SEA, unaltered, through the referendum and ratification process. This sequence was repeated by Mr Ahern, who warned against NATO/PfP in 1995, promised a referendum on it in his 1997 manifesto, and blithely joined, without a referendum, in 1999.

Fianna Fáil's chief contribution to the neutrality debate was perhaps neutralizing opposition by pretending to voice it. This has, however, led to profound disquiet. Four leading party activists wrote to the newspapers deploring the change of policy (*The Irish Times*, 9 June 1999), and another announced the Frank Aiken Society as a forum for those in Fianna Fail who wished to resist it.

> There has been no bottom-up change in FF policy, rather a top-down selling of an unmandated mandarin consensus. (J. Stephenson, *The Irish Times*, 12 June 1999)

Our major parties have effected significant changes in the word and deed of our foreign policy, whilst preventing a clear and open debate on them. When a referendum was forced on them in 1987 they deliberately confounded the issue.

They did this again in 1992. The Maastricht Treaty expanded on the 'European political co-operation' contained in the SEA, setting up:

> a common foreign and security policy [which] shall include all questions related to the security of the Union, including the eventual framing of a common defence policy, which might in time lead to a common defence. (Article J.4.1, in Maguire and Noonan, p. 22)

Paragraph J.4.4 gives another version of the 'reassurance' contained in the SEA, adding that Union policy 'shall not prejudice the specific character of the security and defence policy of certain Member States' (ibid., p. 23). The Irish government claimed this specifically protected Irish neutrality, but during the negotiations they had objected to it. Why they objected becomes clear from the rest of the paragraph: the commitment to respect the obligations of NATO members, and that EU policy shall be 'compatible' with NATO's 'common security and defence policy'. Once again, neither Ireland nor neutrality nor the principle of military alliances is mentioned.

The Amsterdam Treaty proceeded further down the Maastricht road. The commitment remained to a 'common defence policy', which 'might lead to a common defence' (Article J.7 in EU, 1997, p. 12). The phrase 'in time' is dropped, moving 'common defence' more clearly from principle to pragmatic decision. The clause that Union policy shall not prejudice the 'specific character' of certain states' policies is repeated, with again the explicit reference to NATO, prompting the Peace and Neutrality Alliance's query.

> How can 'the policy of the Union ... be compatible with the common security and defence policy established within that framework' (NATO's) and not 'prejudice' the security and defence policies of the neutrals? (PANA, 1998, p. 2)

How can we develop common policies with a group of countries, most of which are in NATO, where the common policy must not conflict with NATO policies, and claim we are preserving the distinction between our principles (neither specifically referred to nor spelt out) and those of NATO? Moreover, the government invoked the EU to justify NATO/PfP membership: they regard the two as intimately linked (Ireland, 1999a, pp. 11-14).

Article J.7 also refers to the Western European Union, which the Maastricht Treaty had called 'an integral part of the development of the Union' (J.4.2, in Ireland, 2001, p. 63). 'Common defence policy' is to be elaborated in the context of the WEU link; we in Ireland had by then become Observers. While Maastricht was being ratified, the WEU held a significant meeting at Petersberg, near Bonn. This produced a range of operations known as the Petersberg Tasks, listed as humanitarian and rescue, peacekeeping and 'tasks of combat forces in crisis management, including peacemaking' (Ireland, 1996, p. 137).

An elaborate choreography between the EU, WEU and NATO produced an alignment between the EU's common policy, evolving in the WEU context, and NATO's approach to the post-Cold War world. For a long time, there had seemed to be two paths of development on the European scene. One was NATO, dating from 1949, and the other was the evolving EEC/EC/EU, which began in 1957 with the Treaty of Rome. There were unresolved issues, with the US at the centre of NATO but not in the EU. Though matters remain fluid in some respects, a great deal of clarity, albeit ominous, has recently emerged.

As NATO's 'Partnership for Peace' gained momentum, it repeatedly offered resources to the EU for precisely those Petersberg Tasks elaborated in the run-up to the Amsterdam Treaty. The new dispensation saw the EU appoint Javier Solana, the NATO Secretary-General, as the 'supremo' to embody its new Common Foreign and Security Policy. It was a quite breathtaking action, at a time when the entire EU Commission had been forced to resign by the European Parliament, and only the new President, Mr Prodi, had been appointed. It was also a hugely symbolic move to select Mr Solana straight from NATO.

Successive governments and oppositions have got us into a fine mess. Staying silent in Brussels rather than spelling out a principled objection to the militarization of the EU, at home they have deflected debate by telling us all that was still to come. Where unable to avoid discussion, they have sown confusion and fear. They allowed EU policy to align itself with the nuclear-armed and increasingly aggressive NATO alliance, whilst denying that this has implications for our previously peace-oriented approach in foreign policy and defence matters.

There have indeed always been people who believed that (a) we should join, for example, NATO and/or (b) joining the EEC implied involvement in military matters. There have, however, been others who disagreed. We are now told that, because various people thought or said various things in the 1950s and onwards, these statements constitute public policy and have legal implications for us now. Democracy is not about what Seán Lemass (or any other leader) 'always thought' or 'always said'; it is about what view of the case is *now explicitly shared by our fellow-citizens*.

A Broken Promise: Ireland Joins NATO/PfP

In 1995 Bertie Ahern opposed the idea of Ireland's joining NATO's new 'Partnership for Peace'. The 1997 manifesto committed his party to a referendum on any such proposal. In 1999, however, he decided to join, refusing a referendum because the Attorney General had advised him that he need not keep his promise! Promises are precisely about things we are not compelled, but give our word, to do.

A breach of trust is all the more disturbing in the specific area of military involvement. This is hugely relevant to the Nice debate, because all the reassurances we are offered about the European Rapid Reaction Force boil down to political promises which can be broken, as was the PfP referendum promise (see pp. 106–121 below). It is beside the point to counter that PfP is not such a big deal anyway: a clear promise about military policy has been publicly broken. It would anyhow be untrue, for PfP has implications for that policy. Mr Ahern in 1995 spoke about 'the NATO Partnership for Peace, a halfway house offering a form of associate membership' (*The Irish Times*, 2 June 1995). He had also warned, in opposition, that any attempt to join without a referendum would be 'a serious breach of faith and fundamentally undemocratic' (Dáil Debates, 28 March 1996).

Though the government tried to distance PfP from NATO, there can be no doubt on the issue. Mr Ahern may ironically be justified in rescinding his 'halfway house' metaphor, and refuting claims that PfP was a 'back door' to NATO: the 50th anniversary edition of the *NATO Handbook* clearly sees it as a front porch:

> The Framework Document also states that active participation in the Partnership for Peace will play an important role in the evolutionary process of including new members in NATO. (NATO, 1999, p. 88)

Operations under NATO/PfP look fairly innocuous: 'peacekeeping, search and rescue, humanitarian operations' (Ireland 1999, p. 36). These are like the WEU Petersberg Tasks endorsed by the EU at Amsterdam. The list differs in omitting the euphemistic 'peacemaking', but concludes with 'others as may subsequently be agreed'. As we will see in discussing the Petersberg Tasks (pp. 107ff. below), there are two problems: the vagueness of the terms themselves, and the fact that the list is open-ended: 'subsequently agreed' by whom, how, when?

Moreover, NATO has longer-term plans for its 'partners'; the final Objective is:

> the development, over the longer term, of forces that are better able to operate with those of the members of the North Atlantic Alliance. (Ireland 1999a, p. 36)

Not only is the entire movement one of drawing 'partners' towards NATO; we have that interesting word, 'operating', rather than 'co-operating', with them. There is clearly no notion of our questioning, let alone altering, the doctrines of this nuclear-based alliance. So much for claims that we would be able to shape things with our expertise in UN peacekeeping: that is quite simply not what it is about.

The two former senior US officials who devised PfP are very clear:

> The objective of a renewed Partnership for Peace should be to make the experience of partnership as close as possible, in practical military terms, to the experience of membership in NATO . . . PfP combined exercises and other military-to-military activities should advance from the partnership's early focus on peacekeeping and humanitarian operations to true combat operations. (Afri, 1999a, p. 9)

NATO, sure as shooting, know where they're going, and where they're bringing anyone who goes along. The US Ambassador to NATO has been quoted as saying that PfP had the aim of 'making the difference between being a partner and being an ally razor thin' (PANA, 1999, p. 2).

NATO Goes to War: the Lessons of Kosovo

If the Gulf War of 1991 was a threshold towards activating the 'new world order', NATO's actions in Serbia/Kosova in 1999 were a gigantic step across that threshold. These actions are highly relevant to emerging EU policy, because of the EU's proximity to, and involvement with, the former Yugoslavia. They are also an object lesson on many of our questions about warfare and international law. Most important for our purposes is their relevance to the Petersberg Tasks.

It is not simply the 'opposition' who link Kosovo with Petersberg. Frederick Bonnart, editor of the independent journal *Nato's Nations*, made the connection soon after the event

(*International Herald Tribune*, 19 November 1999). Arguing for the Nice Treaty in 2001, Daniel Keohane of the Centre for European Reform in London told us 'the bombings in Bosnia and Kosovo are examples of how the resolution of conflicts may require peacemaking operations' (*The Irish Times,* 12 May 2001). John Bruton, in his report for the Oireachtas Joint Committee on European Affairs, spells it out similarly.

> 6.6 While the Petersberg Tasks were accepted on paper, Europe did not have the capacity to perform them . . . NATO undertook the major tasks in Bosnia, and later in Kosovo in enforcing the no-fly zone, in conducting the air strikes and in commanding IFOR and KFOR. (Bruton Report, 2002, p. 58)

We thus have common ground that the Kosovo intervention is a case of what is contemplated as 'peacemaking' under Petersberg. This is the kind of action envisaged by those who supported our moving closer to NATO and now want us to settle into the evolving 'European defence identity'.

The central question about the Serbia/Kosova intervention is: was it right? If we cannot satisfactorily answer that about a given undertaking, we had no business engaging in or supporting it. It is therefore extremely disturbing that the Independent International Commission on Kosovo (IICK) had to be set up on the initiative of the then Prime Minister of Sweden.

> [He was] concerned by the absence of independent analysis of the conflict in Kosovo and any real attempt to research the lessons to be learned from the conflict. (IICK, 2000, p. 21)

We were told at the time that the aim was to put an end to virtual genocide by Milosevic's troops against the Kosovars, and to return displaced people to their homes. Dr Mary Kaldor, though in principle favouring robust interventions, nevertheless was dubious in this case.

> The NATO intervention did not save one Kosovar Albanian. On the contrary, it provided a cover under which the Serbs accelerated ethnic cleansing [sic]. (*Observer*, 18 July 1999.)

A similar criticism was made by Lord Carrington, a former Secretary-General of NATO itself (*The Times*, 27 August 1999). The IICK, reporting over a year later, reached the following conclusion:

> The NATO air campaign did not provoke the attacks on the civilian Kosovar population but the bombing created an environment that made such an operation feasible . . .[;] the intervention failed to achieve its avowed aim of preventing massive ethnic cleansing [sic] . . . [,] it was also a serious mistake by the NATO countries not to foresee that the bombing would lead to severe attacks on the Albanian population. (IICK, 2000, pp. 3, 97, 89; see also p. 93.)

To argue thus does not seek to shift the blame for the Kosovo slaughter from Milosevic or from his willing executioners. Indeed, the very suggestion that we might so wish betrays a woeful lack of moral reflection on the part of those who advance it.

There are also serious questions about the co-ordination and control exercised over specific tactics. BBC TV's *Newsnight* on 20 August 1999 reported:

> On the 30th of March, Mr Solana, General Clark and General Naumann jointly informed NATO Ambassadors that the old phased war plan with its political safeguards was being thrown away. In return for a promise that NATO would only hit 'strictly military targets' the lukewarm allies were then persuaded to back them. General Clark then hit the Milosevic Party HQ, the Presidential Palace, and the TV stations – all targets taken from the phase-three list that several allies had refused to vote for . . . The subsequent bombing of electrical power plants disabled the pumps without which water supplies

were disconnected, and put out of action vital equipment in hospitals. (Coates, 1999, pp. 7-8)

We must also consider the vexed question of high-altitude bombing, designed to avoid NATO casualties. This seems to have contributed significantly to the number of occasions when civilian casualties suffered 'collateral damage'.

> In spite of the fact that NATO made substantial [efforts] to avoid civilian casualties there were some serious mistakes. Some 500 civilian deaths are documented. (IICK, 2000, p. 5)

Air strikes against civilian infrastructure 'contradicted initial NATO assurances that the war was not aimed at the Serbian people' (ibid., p.93). The picture, of incompetence and confusion bordering on the purely reckless, gets worse as the IICK attempts to ascertain NATO's motives for the intervention. Central to these was the commitment to that deadly oxymoron, 'threat diplomacy' (e.g., ibid., p. 4).

> The reasons behind US and NATO inflexibility extended beyond the issue of Kosovo. NATO was seeking to clarify its longer-term mandate after the end of the Cold War, and the upcoming fiftieth anniversary scheduled for April 1999 was to be a key step in this process. Closely related, the reliance on threat diplomacy was at odds with any wavering on the part of NATO. In other words, a threat to use force so as to achieve an outcome that is non-negotiable, i.e. NATO peacekeeping force in Kosovo, is inconsistent with any indication that some alternative compromise is possible. Negotiations in the sense of actual bargaining would seem inconsistent and costly to the credibility of NATO as a political actor. (ibid., pp. 157-8)

Our concerns whether NATO was doing 'the right thing' are thus compounded by the evidence that whatever it did was done substantially 'for the wrong reason'.

The situation regarding *legality* is on the face of it clear: even if a state is acting in self-defence it needs to operate with continuing explicit reference to the UN Security Council. Any other threat or use of force, not sanctioned directly by the Security Council, is illegal under the UN Charter. The IICK is succinct in its judgment:

> it remains difficult to reconcile NATO's recourse to armed intervention on behalf of Kosovo with the general framework of legal rights and duties which determines the legality of the use of force. (IICK, 2000, p. 167)

Some argue that international law has moved on from the post-1945 dispensation, with new rights and obligations now in place alongside – even sometimes overruling – the principle of non-intervention; there is an account of the overall debate in chapter 6 of the report. This concludes that the action was illegal, for three reasons: the failure to seek, let alone receive, Security Council authorization; the failure, given a perceived *impasse* within the Council, to seek authority from the General Assembly under the rubric of 'uniting for peace', and the absence in NATO's own charter, the Washington Treaty, of grounds for forceful action other than in self-defence (ibid., p.166; see also Glennon, 2001).

The IICK goes on to detail why, despite any legitimacy it may have had, the illegal intervention was at best imprudent. The argument that NATO needed to act because of UN weakness was:

> somewhat self-serving, as the earlier UN failure was partly a result of the refusal by the NATO countries to support the Bosnian effort in a more vigorous and effective manner. (ibid., pp. 170, 175)

Let us assume humanitarian concerns were the sole motive for the intervention; *this made UN authorization more crucially necessary than ever*. Here was the self-styled 'international community' deciding to ignore the taboo on intervention within and against a sovereign state's territory. To establish legitimacy for the intervention, to distinguish it from the imperialist gunboat diplomacy it so closely resembled, should have been a crucial priority (see IICK, 2000, p. 189).

Having found the NATO intervention illegal under international law, it is at first sight surprising that the IICK suggests a sense in which the action was 'illegal but legitimate' (ibid., p. 4).

> [T]he Commission takes the view that the pattern of Serb oppression in Kosovo, the experience of ethnic cleansing [sic] a few years earlier in Bosnia, and the lack of international response to genocide in Rwanda in 1994 combine to create a strong moral and political duty on the part of the international community to act effectively, and to express solidarity with civilian societies victimized by governments guilty of grave breaches of human rights ... [The Kosovo] situation supports the general conclusion that the NATO campaign was illegal, yet legitimate. (ibid., pp. 185-6)

The IICK clearly sees such legitimacy as highly restricted and problematic. It makes the general point that '[a]llowing this gap between legality and legitimacy to persist is not healthy, for several reasons' (ibid., p. 186).

These reasons are spelt out most usefully by considering whether the NATO intervention was morally *necessary*, in the sense that the problem could not have been addressed in any other way. The IICK's analysis shows that the intervention can be seen as 'legitimate' only in the light of immediate circumstances arising in turn from the failure to tackle the problem effectively in the preceding longer term. The story of the build-up to the Serbia/Kosova action in March 1999 is thus a dreadful parable of failure to apply the cogent analysis of the spectrum from causes to consequences so well spelt out by Erskine Childers III in March 1995 (see pp. 44 ff. above).

The report notes a strong option for non-violence among the Kosovars in the 1980s and 1990s, when they set up social and governmental structures of their own, including a quite complex educational system, health care, courts and other elements. Not only were those initiatives not effectively engaged with by the EU and NATO; on the contrary, these latter, when focusing on Bosnia-Herzegovina, quite markedly sidelined Kosovo, which did not even appear on the agenda for the Dayton talks with Milosevic.

Diplomacy had clearly not been exhausted. True, talks broke down at Rambouillet, but they broke down over demands made by NATO. These involved a degree of submission by the Serbs, in their own territory, which amounted to a provocation to any sovereign state, and also an adamant insistence by NATO that they, rather than the UN, should have control of the peacekeeping operation.

> If NATO had initiated an offer to relent on the implementation provisions, Serbia would have lost a fundamental excuse for not signing on. (IICK, 2000, p. 157; see also ibid., pp. 140-1, and Skidelsky, 1999, pp. 13-15)

We have already looked into the standard argument why UN approval is not sought because Russia and/or China would deny it. Would we accept our government doing something without necessary Dáil approval because it feared it might lose a vote?

The very word 'humanitarian' has become tainted and possibilities of human rights enforcement have become entangled with issues of nation-state aggrandizement. We are left in a situation where NATO countries will carry little conviction in dissuading other states from pursuing what they choose to call humanitarian concerns in what they choose to see as their spheres of interest (see IICK, 2000, pp. 174-5).

That raising these questions is not an excuse for inaction is argued most eloquently by Robert Skidelsky:

> In the last few weeks I have often been asked: 'But would you have just stood idly by and done nothing?' This assumes that there were no alternatives to what

> was actually done. But had the concept of 'damage limitation' rather than punishing Serbia been the lodestar of the diplomatic efforts, a whole range of alternatives would have disclosed itself – from economic sanctions or even bribes to making sure that an enlarged force of UN and OSCE monitors were kept on the ground. If there is one thing which history teaches us it is that monstrous acts can only be performed in dark places away from prying eyes... in fact the evidence is that, once the monitors entered Kosovo in October 1998, the level of violence fell off: they were withdrawn, of course, once bombing became imminent. There was always a trade-off between prolonged but troubled peace under the watchful eye of the world and the evils of war under the protection of an informational blackout. (Skidelsky, 1999, pp. 17-18)

The IICK endorses this view of the effectiveness of the OSCE monitors (IICK, pp. 150-1), and also more generally of the lost opportunities for patient engagement:

> The inadequacy of diplomatic efforts in the period 1997-8 was to culminate eventually with Rambouillet where the space for maneuver was extremely limited. (ibid., p. 63)

The manic focusedness of war makes people least receptive to what they most need to hear, just when they most need to hear it. This became evident quite early in the bombing campaign when various appalling blunders had occurred and Milosevic had not quickly given in. From political leaders in Britain, the US and elsewhere we began to hear the mantra, 'NATO must and will prevail'. These leaders quite clearly, with seeming rationality, argued they were fighting simply in order to win: victory was the only exit strategy.

The madness of war confers a seeming authority on the wielders of weapons. Even those who in no way agree with them are silenced, stunned by the sheer awesomeness of what is being done. To impress in this way, to shift us from reason to power, is part of the point of weapons in the first place. One of the grave costs of our failure to think and talk enough about war in times of relative peace is our reluctance to believe that those wielding the weapons would do so for any but the best motives, under any but the most compelling of circumstances. This is nowhere more painfully evident than in the recent crisis between India and Pakistan. The problem is that those who initiate the military action are also the arbiters of its rightness and necessity, and the deeper we get into a war-situation, the less possibility is there of effective scrutiny or dissent.

In discussing Irish policy, we would clearly have ample grounds for concern over all these questions about NATO's actions in spring 1999; these are amplified by our government's broken promise on joining NATO/PfP in late 1999. We would be right, then, to worry lest the Kosovo intervention be the kind of thing an Irish government might persuade itself to endorse in the future. In reality, the situation is far worse: *the Irish government actually endorsed the NATO action at the time!*

Our government signed a Statement of the European Council on the Kosovo in March 1999. This Statement referred to the EU's responsibility:

> for securing peace and cooperation in the region which will guarantee the respect of our basic European values, i.e. the respect of human and minority rights, international law, democratic institutions and the inviolability of borders. (EU, 1999, p. 2.)

The Statement presented Rambouillet as an all-out attempt to find a negotiated settlement that would be 'fair for both parties to the conflict'.

> The international community has done its utmost to find a peaceful solution to the Kosovo conflict. (ibid., p.1)

The IICK has found, as many argued at the time, that these claims are false. Our government chose to ignore the clear evidence that other means had not been exhausted before NATO decided to bomb and that it had so decided without seeking Security Council authorization. Our diplomatic service is rightly well regarded for its competence; nobody can claim that the Irish government simply 'didn't know'.

I do not agree with the heaping of scorn on our then Minister for Foreign Affairs for his observation that the crisis put us 'between a rock and a hard place'. This lucidly conveyed the dilemma of being unhappy with a crucial action by powerful nations with whom we are on friendly terms. Many are fellow-members of the EU and one of them, the US, had played a major role in the emergence of the Good Friday Agreement. We were in that sense between a rock and a hard place. Unfortunately, we then decided that we would be better off under the rock.

Our government was prepared or felt compelled so to act while still a non-member of NATO/PfP and before a common European policy has been fully elaborated. This leaves no grounds for confidence that we can 'influence things from the inside' as we are so often encouraged to do. Surely we in Ireland have particular reason to worry when problematic notions of legitimacy can trump those of legality; what was the 1970 Arms Trial about? What price our concern at home with vigilantism if we are unconcerned about who precisely carries out 'legitimate' interventions and on what legal or illegal grounds?

This points up the inconsistency between the stance of politicians like Mr Ahern and Mr Blair on the question of conflict in this country and their attitude to the conflict in the former Yugoslavia. The first sets its face resolutely against even the suspicion that armed force can produce a real resolution of political conflicts, whilst the second seeks to bomb the Serbs to the negotiating table. The IICK has pointed out that one of the bitterest fruits of NATO's actions is the lesson 'that violence is an effective way to achieve political objectives' (IICK, 2000, p. 64; see also ibid., p. 149).

Not only is this highly regrettable; it also sits very ill with Article 29.2 of our Constitution, which states:

> Ireland affirms its adherence to the principle of the pacific settlement of international disputes by international arbitration or judicial determination. (Ireland, 1999b, p. 108)

Not only this. How can we develop the doctrine, first spelt out at Nuremberg, that there is no defence of 'only obeying orders', if we are prepared to subscribe to false declarations like the above simply on grounds of political or diplomatic embarrassment? My concern relates to our share of the blame for what NATO did with this EU endorsement and to the shame of our not having had the moral courage to do something to thwart it, or at least deny it the pretence of moral necessity.

There is one apparently crushing rejoinder to all these arguments. The Kosovo report was written before Milosevic fell from power: maybe the NATO bombardment worked after all? Even if such a cause/effect link could be established, that would not answer the IICK's suggestion that things might have gone quite differently if earlier non-violent opposition had been supported. They talk about links between dissident Serbian and Kosovar intellectuals before the KLA had emerged in strength, and common ground between students as well.

> Indeed, the students in Belgrade were making contact with the students in Prishtina/Pristina; the Post-Pessimists' club for example, developed branches throughout Yugoslavia. (IICK, 2000, p. 54)

Around that time Belgrade students set up Otpor! to oppose Milosevic.

> NATO bombs provided further serious interference with opposition activity and protest, but still support for Otpor! grew – internationally as well. (Peace Matters, 2001-02, p. 8)

Why do we learn of these green shoots only when the dust of the 'daisy-cutters' begins to settle? Surely some of the resources and ingenuity that went into NATO's war would have protected and nurtured them? Even if we confidently assert that the bombardment 'succeeded', it would be at the cost of its immoral tactics, its evident illegality and, worst of all, its message that 'violence works'. This leads us directly to the option between systematic warfare and peace process, and their respective implications for our world.

Peace Process or 'War on Terrorism'?

> We call upon the governments and peoples of the world to take concrete steps in developing a Culture of Peace and Non-violence. The response of the US and its allies should not be driven by a blind desire for vengeance, but rather a renewed determination to work for a peaceful and just world. The single evil that must be opposed is not one group of people or another, but rather the fear and hatred that continue to find root in human hearts. (Nobel Peace Laureates, 2001)

The early 1990s offered a window of opportunity; it seems now that we may have not only missed that window, but demolished the building that contained it. The new conventional wisdom is that by destroying people, and their physical and social environment, we can make the world safe for peace, as though peace were a distant future which could be achieved only through its own negation. This has huge implications for us in Ireland. Our long history has been an agonizing lesson in the effects and the limitations – moral and practical – of violence. The development of democracy has been intertwined, throughout the island, with the question of legitimate force.

The peace process of the past 10 years has challenged all of us, including the states involved, and brought a growing consensus on the following points:

- violence is an assault on the life and well-being of our fellow-citizens and their community;

- the effect of that violence is not restricted to its most direct impact in immediate injury and death: it leaves a legacy of sorrow, hurt and resentment;
- nobody can healthily imagine their own future, let alone the place of others in it, under the impact or threat of violence;
- we have to dig deep in our assumptions and practices if we are to move beyond merely regretting violence and invent our way out of it;
- this frequently involves not reacting forcefully, even when we feel we would be 'justified' to do so, in order to build up a momentum for non-violence.

These principles had informed a coherent approach to international affairs of which we were legitimately proud. There is every danger now that we may stamp them 'not for export' just when the world needs small, confident societies like ours to stand up for our beliefs. It is particularly ironic that this should be done in the belief that it helps friendly countries, particularly the United States, which have played such a role in proclaiming them in our peace process. When Minister of State for Foreign Affairs Liz O'Donnell told her Progressive Democrat colleagues that 'the apparatus and mentality of war had also to be decommissioned' (*The Irish Times*, 11 February 2002), was that message for home consumption only?

The problem about such inconsistency lies too deep for point-scoring. It is not that we are doing the right thing in one place but the wrong one in others; we are not actually doing what we thought we were doing in the first place. Our claim that our actions flow from a particular moral premise cannot be valid because that premise obtains elsewhere and yet our action does not flow. It is always worthwhile to learn from our actions what are our actual, rather than our fantasized, principles. These may well be perfectly respectable, but not necessarily so.

The inconsistencies of Western policy are hugely instructive and scarcely edifying. We seem quite ready to give military, financial and 'moral' support to grotesque figures and groups, many of whom we soon afterwards promote to 'least favoured terrorist' status, without ever apparently learning the lesson. We bomb in one region because people are being killed, whilst at the very same time ignoring the vastly greater numbers being slaughtered elsewhere (Shawcross, 2000, p. 324).

UN resolutions are stretched to breaking point to bomb one country for allegedly possessing weapons of mass destruction, the bombing being carried out by the inventors and chief possessors of such weapons, who turn a blind eye to their proliferation in other places (see Halliday and von Sponeck, 2000). We launch wars to deal with the utterly predictable consequences of pumping arms-for-profit into the very countries we then attack in the name of peace. No wonder that P.J. O'Rourke should tickle our funny bone with his cynical title, *Give War a Chance* – but is he all that cynical?

How different would the world look if we were indeed openly 'giving war a chance'? Are we all by now so inured to absurdity that we patronizingly dismiss an appeal such as that of Ryan Amundson, whose brother died in the Pentagon?

> Working to stop conditions which breed hate may be more complex and difficult than just dropping bombs, but the existence of evil does not have an easy solution.
> (Ryan Amundson, 2001, p. 3)

It is vital to reappraise the 'practical, hard-headed realism' of those who would call him naïve. If we do not, we are accepting that the rhetoric of our peace process is, like certain medicines, for local application only, with a health warning: do not inhale! What has been achieved here would then stand not as a small but promising start, but as a convenient region of managed peace in a larger scenario of acceptable violence.

We have so far in this essay looked at the considerations that ought to govern any use of defensive force and at some of the consequences of our failure to implement them in our contemporary world. The result is a situation where war seems to have been adopted as the answer to our problems – the reliable provider, rather than the enemy, of peace. We have seen this in the EU's self-characterization as well as in the US's (see p. 33 above).

This downgrades the most basic principle of the UN Charter, which commits it *before all else* 'to save succeeding generations from the scourge of war' (UN, 2001, p.3). The Charter goes on to detail human rights, equal dignity of all persons and of nations large and small, respect for international law, and social progress in freedom as the concomitants of abolishing war. Now these priorities are being stood on their head. For example, in an eloquent conspectus of the challenges of the twenty-first century, Bill Clinton tells us:

> Victory for our point of view depends upon four things. First, we have to win the fight we're in, in Afghanistan and against these terrorist networks that threaten us today. (*Irish Examiner*, 18 December 2001)

Lord, make us peaceful – but not today. This is the language of a world addicted to violence: just one more little war for the road to peace.

'These terrorist networks' – a touch of President Bush's folksiness – brings to mind Niall O'Dowd's condemnation of critics of US policies. I criticized his argument, but said there was one central part of it which, if valid, could perhaps rescue much or most of it. This is his depiction of the danger presented by bin Laden, al-Qa'ida and, indeed, Islamic fundamentalism in general. This threat, he believes, not merely justifies but requires a 'War on Terrorism'.

Some Muslim writers have indeed made points similar to Niall O'Dowd's. Ziauddin Sardar, for example, has asked:

> Why have we repeatedly turned a blind eye to the evil within our societies? . . . Muslims are quick to note the double standards of America . . . But we seldom question our own double standards . . . The psychotic young

> men ... shouting fascist obscenities outside the Pakistan Embassy, are enjoying the fruits of Western freedom of expression ... [;] in any self-proclaimed Islamic state, they would be ruthlessly silenced. (*Observer*, 23 November 2001)

The Iraqi dissident Kanan Makiya has suggested that the valid grievances of the Arab and Muslim world have become overlaid by:

> continuing to wallow in one's own victimhood to the point of losing the essentially universal idea of human dignity and worth that is the only true measure of civility ... Attribution of all of the ills of one's own world to either the great Satan, America, or the little one, Israel ... became the legitimising cement upon which such murderous regimes as Saddam Hussein's Iraq were built. (*Observer*, 7 October 2001)

No recital of grievances can justify our picking on persons, known or unknown, to be 'taken out' of the human family. Nothing, equally, excuses subjecting others to the life-corroding fear of such a fate. Sardar and Makiya rightly argue that the Islamic world must take responsibility on this score.

Yet O'Dowd's argument differs significantly from theirs. He is right that the world faces a huge danger from the likes of bin Laden, and associated regimes such as the Taliban are an affront to any worthwhile political values. One is made uneasy, however, by how he advances the argument. His prescription is, as we have seen, not merely war, but war without the 'Queensbury Rules'. This vehemence is fuelled by his image of the enemy as:

> Islamic fundamentalism, as vicious as any fascism that Hitler practised ... Bin Laden and al-Qaeda are the Hitler and Wehrmacht of this generation, bent on mass destruction, and to pretend otherwise is ridiculous. (*The Irish Times*, 19 December 2001)

The last six words of this quotation are merely heat masquerading as light. It is also significant that he invokes the ultimate thought-stopper of Hitler's Nazism, one of those regimes so awful that we would not even wish to fantasize worse. What is not so clear is whether invoking it as the last word on current trends in the Muslim and Arab world helps matters greatly.

Is this to justify what O'Dowd condemns? No. Whilst we need to understand acts of terror in relation to their circumstances, these are not a justification. Equally, we need not be Sigmund Freud to question the urge to locate evil as 'them over there'. That urge distorts our view of ourselves and of those we condemn. It also ignores Sardar's request that the rest of the world 'could help by adopting a more balanced tone' rather than depicting the US as 'a personification of innocence and goodness'. O'Dowd admits the US has had its faults, but only in the past, and brooks no criticism of its present policies and actions.

Sardar and Makiya also differ significantly in their views from O'Dowd and his notion of how the threat of Muslim extremism is to be met.

> To every Muslim everywhere I issue this fatwa: any Muslim involved in the planning, financing, training, recruiting, support or harbouring of those who commit acts of indiscriminate violence against persons or the apparatus or infrastructure of states is guilty of terror and no part of the *ummah* [the Muslim world community]. It is the duty of every Muslim to spare no effort in hunting down, apprehending and bringing such criminals to justice. (Sardar, *Observer*, 23 November 2001)

> Muslims and Arabs have to be on the front lines of a new kind of war, one that is worth waging for their own salvation and in their own souls. And that, as good out-of-fashion Muslim scholars will tell you, is the true meaning of *jihad*, a meaning that has been hijacked by terrorists and suicide bombers and all those who applaud or find excuses for them. To exorcise what they have done in our name is the civilisational challenge of the twenty-first century for every Arab and Muslim in the world today. (Makiya, *Observer*, 7 October 2001)

Both of our Muslim writers, then, place the central responsibility on Muslims themselves for this struggle towards reason in a world of grievance.

Makiya, admittedly, puts this so strongly that he sets up the mirror image of the 'victimhood' he so rightly rejects.

> To argue, as many Arabs and Muslims are doing today (and not a few liberal Western voices), that 'Americans should ask themselves why they are so hated in the world' . . . bolsters the project of the perpetrators of the heinous act of 11 September, which is to blur the lines that separate their sect of a few hundred people from hundreds of millions of peace-loving Muslims and Arabs. (ibid.)

Sometimes the beam in our own eye, when we focus on it exclusively, can blind us to that in the eyes of others. Can the relatives of the victims of 11 September, who have asked the forbidden question, be dismissed as among merely 'a few liberal Western voices'? This would be, in the Irish context, to see Gordon Wilson's prophetic charity, on the loss of his beloved daughter in the Enniskillen bombing, as somehow endorsing the viciousness which had injured him in so many ways.

We become adults precisely to the extent that we realize we are neither totally pure victims nor totally impure monsters; the claim of total culpability is as distorting as the claim of total innocence. Makiya, by his exclusive emphasis on the fascist tendencies of Muslim fundamentalism, can hardly intend to exculpate, for example, those Hindu extremists who have wrought such horrors on Muslims in Gujarat in India in early 2002.

The equation of fundamentalism with Hitler's Nazism has massive historical resonances for all groups confronting them, above all in the conflict between the Palestinians and Zionism. I will not attempt to summarize that conflict, or to trace all the pathways of pain that it has followed. We are also, I hope, beyond the need to balance out one shattered Israeli life or family against another shattered Palestinian one; the question is how the culture and practice of violence can be replaced by a genuine culture and practice of peace.

One can draw some encouragement from the fact that this very question has been creatively and courageously posed from within Israeli society itself. Prime Minister Sharon has not commanded unanimous support with his prescription:

> We are in a hard war with a cruel and bloodthirsty enemy. We must cause the Palestinians losses, casualties, so that they understand they will gain nothing by terrorism. We must hit them, and hit them again and again, until they understand. (*Observer*, 10 March 2002)

These three sentences will repay frequent rereading, for they lucidly display the futility of policies of violence. It is far from facetious to observe that their kind of pedagogy teaches, not the lesson that is allegedly intended, but the lesson that violence is the only or best way to move minds.

A different message has come from Ometz le-Sarev, the movement of 'refuseniks' who will not carry out military service in the occupied territories.

> Not only have they all worn the country's uniform, but they are the men in their 20s and 30s the Israeli army regards as its new generation of commanders . . . They adamantly believe in a Jewish state – they just want no part in ruling over another people . . . Even their critics have to concede that these men are motivated by love of country . . . And so Israel has to listen . . . No one can close their ears to this testimony, crying media bias or anti-semitism. These are Israel's soldiers speaking, in their own words. Israel's former attorney-general, Michael Ben-Yair, says: 'History's verdict will be that their refusal was the act that restored our moral backbone.' (Jonathan Freedland, *Guardian*, 6 March 2002)

Michael Ben-Yair has indeed gone further, in an analysis which addresses the power configuration between Israelis and Palestinians, even calling the Palestinian *intifada* a war of national liberation.

> We enthusiastically chose to become a colonialist society, ignoring international treaties, expropriating lands, transferring settlers from Israel to the occupied territories, engaging in theft and finding justification for all these activities . . . we established an apartheid regime. (*Guardian*, 11 April 2002)

I am writing in the week when Israeli troops have, apparently, moved out of the refugee town of Jenin and the world has begun to see some of what was wrought there in the previous few weeks. It seems impossible that the verdict on these actions will be anything less than severe condemnation and it is to be hoped that a proper inquiry will have been carried out by the time these words are published. We already know enough to say that the Israeli actions amounted to a systematic violation of the basic principles that should govern the use of force. David Holley, an independent expert military observer for Amnesty International, concluded:

> The military operations we have investigated appear to be carried out not for military purposes but instead to harass, humiliate, intimidate and harm the Palestinian population. Either the Israeli army is extremely ill-disciplined or it has been ordered to carry out acts which violate the laws of war. (Amnesty advertisement, *The Irish Times*, 27 April 2002)

Israel had refused to let observers monitor what it was doing, and ignored the decisions of the UN Security Council. It then excluded journalists and Red Cross/Red Crescent personnel during crucial actions in April 2002 on the spurious grounds that it did not want them to be casualties in crossfire: that risk is part of their job. This is all the more disquieting, given how the rhetoric of 'rooting out terrorists' was combined with an onslaught on the very life-world of the Palestinian people.

During this onslaught, Mr Sharon has frequently intoned the mantra that he is only enacting the script laid down by his mentors in the 'War on Terrorism'. The point is well taken. When asked whether Israel's difficulties justify its actions in Palestinian places, the British Chief Rabbi said the same.

> What is happening now is the direct equivalent of what America is doing in Afghanistan. (*Today*, BBC Radio 4, 17 April 2002)

There is little point in trying to justify Israeli government actions as a surgical excision of the terrorist evil when we see the indiscriminate actions their strategy has produced. This is a central problem in the rhetoric of the 'War on Terrorism' and its associated demonization not merely of evildoers but of the world they inhabit. To maintain that the world just happens to be divided into good people who are inexplicably victimized and bad people who inexplicably commit crimes of violence risks condemning us all to a world and a lifetime of war.

One cannot write these words without sensing the frustration of those who will say, with Niall O'Dowd, that you can't fight terrorism and observe the niceties. Yet prudence, if nothing more, dictates that we ask is it feasible to thwart all those bent on violence by overwhelming force, without producing a new cohort of righteous martyrs. Tony Benn has suggested that we face two kinds of corruption: not only the corruption of power, but also that of *powerlessness* (Benn, p. 11). This latter needs to be tackled by stern justice towards the perpetrators, rather than harsh vengeance on their loosely defined associates; the box-cutter does not justify the 'daisy-cutter'. It also requires addressing the underlying powerlessness, which cannot be done without creative action by the powerful.

No country is better placed to alter this scenario than the USA. Its every word and deed have a resonance almost beyond imagining. We long for it to realize the positive freedoms that this position opens up for it, and to embrace their possibilities. This is why, well before 11 September, it was so frustrating and alarming to see it plan to transmute its colossal energies into overwhelming power, forgetting the words of one of its own finest poets, Conrad Aiken:

> Perpetual strength is as much a weakness as perpetual weakness.

His outlook is far from that of the US military authorities, in their Joint Vision 2020:

> For the joint force of the future, this goal will be achieved through full spectrum dominance – the ability of US forces, operating unilaterally or in combination with multinational and interagency partners, to defeat any adversary and control any situation across the full range of military operations . . . The label Full Spectrum Dominance implies that US forces are able to conduct prompt, sustained, and synchronised operations . . . in all domains – space, sea, land, air and information. (Quoted, Coates, 2002, p. 6; full text in *The Spokesman*, no. 67, 2000, pp. 31–42)

At heart, this says that the US military will be able to control, and if necessary defeat, all comers at all times.

> Last Spring . . . Richard Cheney informed the press that 'the arrangement [for] the twenty-first century is most assuredly being shaped right now . . . The United States will continue to be the dominant political, economic and military power in the world.' (It is interesting how, when they hear these words, most US-Americans take them as an affirmation and are unable to project their imagination into the meanings of the word 'dominant', as if being domin*ated* in the nuclear and post-modern age was not a painful and life-threatening experience.) (Gerson, 2002b, pp. 2-3).

It is tempting to seek such power – if one pessimistically concludes that there is no other way to promote one's interests – but it exacts a price in squandered energies and constant escalation. The establishment think-tank, the RAND Corporation, describes missile defence as 'not simply a shield but an enabler of action' (quoted, Chomsky, 2001, p. 10; see also Arkin, 2002).

> Russia has also published a new security document, in which the military doctrine governing the use of nuclear

> weapons... has a closer resemblance to the NATO doctrine of 'first strike' in that it sanctions their use against conventional attack. (Brennan, 2000, pp. 7-8)

While the post-Cold War 'window' was still ajar, the Warsaw Pact disbanded and Russia accepted a raft of Western arms-control measures. These and other promising moves have been nullified by the decision to expand NATO, rather than build collective European security through the UN/OSCE. Much has been made of the fact that countries like the Czech Republic have joined NATO. Their reasoning reflects this lost opportunity.

> In the early period after the fall of the Berlin Wall, some of the Eastern European states, former members of the Warsaw Pact, initially favoured the idea of a pan-European security body. They changed their minds when they understood the US position. (Blackaby, 1996, p. 4)

Emerging Eastern European countries were swept up in NATO expansion, thus once more defining European 'security' in terms of fault-lines and confrontation.

> If, as NATO plans and expects, Russia falls into its embrace, the alliance is on track to become (and don't think the Chinese and the Islamic world have not noticed) not only a security system that reaches from Los Angeles to Vladivostok, but something more ambitious still: the white race in arms (Martin Walker, *Guardian*, 27 October 1998).

NATO's expansion has also stretched well into former Soviet Asia, enacting former US National Security Adviser Zbigniew Brzezinski's vision of Eurasia as the key to world dominance.

> Peace movements, in their weakened state, paid some attention to the eastward expansion of NATO, and often opposed the subversion of the neutrals, but they largely ignored the eastward progress of the Partnership for Peace [in] the Ukraine, Georgia and some of the most important Central Asian republics. (Coates, 2002a, p. 1)

One horror of the past decade has been our forced lesson in geography, as violence stains one region of our globe after another. Thinkers like Brzezinski have been quite clear that this process has a material basis. The key was in fact geology, as spelt out by Christian Caryl, Moscow Bureau Chief of *Newsweek*:

> Before the attacks in New York and Washington, Central Asia figured in policy debates primarily because of 'pipeline politics' – the geopolitical competition between states for the region's huge oil and gas resources. Now ... Central Asia has suddenly leaped beyond the concerns of the oilmen, the diplomats and the academics. The US military is building a lasting presence in Uzbekistan, Kyrgyzstan, and perhaps Tajikistan as well ... and this development is already causing unease in Moscow, Beijing, and the Central Asian countries themselves. (Caryl, 2002, p. 27)

One of the architects of this networking was General Zinni, more recently a US 'peace envoy' in Palestine. It should interest us here that:

> The United States spent much of the 1990s cultivating military-to-military ties in Central Asia within the frame of the NATO Partnership for Peace program. (ibid.)

At least we're not alone!

There are many who now sincerely doubt that the US is best serving itself, or world peace, by its posture in the current 'War on Terrorism'. Not only is its characterization of Islamic fundamentalism problematic; its support of many detested and repressive regimes, which that fundamentalism opposes, is unsavoury and ironically risks the 'blowback' of recruiting growing numbers for its proclaimed enemy.

> Sadly, the forceful new US presence in Central Asia, and its seemingly unconditional antiterrorist alliance with the dictators, could well end up dealing a final blow to regional dreams of pluralism ... And that, paradoxically ... will end up driving the discontented

toward the only political alternatives that are radical enough to put up a fight. (Caryl, 2002, p. 29)

A similar warning has been issued by the administrator of the UN Development Programme (see Mark Malloch Brown, in *Independent on Sunday*, 11 November 2001).

We are of course tempted to dismiss our enemies, even to see them as the incarnation of all that is bad. We must consider whether it is prudent to write off a huge and growing section of a major world culture as evil, beyond dispute or dialogue. To anathematize all the energies that currently express themselves in Islamic fundamentalism is – at the very least – a high-risk strategy for the West. It fails to grasp to what extent that fundamentalism is a despairing protest at so many repressive and corrupt regimes maintained in Islamic countries by Western arms, money and 'moral' support.

We in the West often speak of fundamentalism as though viewing a distant jungle from an enlightened conservatory. We overlook the huge and increasing role played in our societies, and their leadership, by Christian fundamentalists. We also miss, more generally, how our 'rational, secular' civilization often looks from the outside – for example, the daily human sacrifice to the economic 'fundamentals' decreed by the IMF and World Bank.

We claim a world-view that every right-thinking person shares, or should share, or can be made to share. We are unconvincing in accusing others of imposing their beliefs by force and fear, given the indiscriminate ways we ascribe and avenge 'terrorism'. Are we, then, the incarnation of evil? No: there is none or, if there is, it is the human species, which is also the incarnation of whatever good and hope we possess, which we need better to cherish.

This discussion of the 'War on Terrorism' is no digression from our theme of EU defence policy and Ireland's relation to it. As we have seen in preceding discussions, the EU's policy has evolved within, shaping and shaped by, the context of NATO's new doctrines and eastward expansion. These are the strands from which the new defence thinking has been woven, culminating in the 'War on Terrorism'. Not only has the EU, as we have seen, taken on much of the language of that project in its recent rhetoric. Our last government put Shannon Airport at the disposal of US warplanes, without a debate on the implications of this for Dáil Eireann's constitutional jurisdiction over warfare.

Mr Ahern went to Washington and, revelling in his privileged access to Mr Bush's ear, declared that Ireland would support the campaign 'in every way open to us' (*The Irish Times*, 13 March 2002). Deaglán de Bréadún reflected concern about these departures:

> Ireland did not take direct part in the Afghan war, but it held America's coat . . . Even among those who broadly supported the Afghan war, there is some concern that proper procedures may not have been followed. With the state entering into commitments to take part in the European Rapid Reaction Force, there is more than the usual anxiety about adhering to the rules. (*The Irish Times*, 29 December 2001)

This image of Ireland as 'coat-holder' smacks ironically of that very hypocrisy our establishment is always so ready to ascribe to its opponents.

Ireland has peculiar reason to note the ironies involved. The entire logic of the Irish peace process is at odds with the approach NATO's leaders – including key architects of the peace process – have promoted in the past decade. We need to submit our international relations to the same scrutiny that the advocates of non-violence directed onto the national question here for years. We need to insist that aggressive solutions, whether they apparently work or not, are wrong because a decent, respectful world cannot be built on them.

What makes these incontrovertible principles in Ireland, yet prevents them from informing and ruling our attitude to international relations (see Kenny, 2001)? Is it wrong to undermine talks with violence here, but right to bomb Milosevic (or rather his oppressed fellow-citizens) into acceptance of the more provocative details of NATO's agenda? Is it right to take seriously those who object to associating with even a suspicion of armed force, whilst joining in a 'partnership' which allows peacekeeping and humanitarianism to be redefined and dominated by an aggressive nuclear military alliance?

When Mo Mowlam said that 'all violence, for whatever reason it is perpetrated, is unacceptable' (*The Irish Times*, 27 August 1999), what was the scope of her pronouncement? In the Northern Ireland context it seems to mean that violence is simply out; though you cannot avoid a few dreadful 'dying kicks', you regard them as unnecessary and unjustified, and the world would be better if they had never happened. Nobody could so interpret NATO's intervention in former Yugoslavia. The grotesqueness of this conjuncture was best captured by a caller to RTÉ Radio's *Tonight with Vincent Browne*, who described the NATO operation in Kosovo as 'a punishment beating'.

Are we now to support a global re-enactment of internment without trial, sensory deprivation, shoot-to-kill policies, and the repeated insistence that 'right' will triumph militarily over 'evil', with not one mention of the sources from which the undoubted, but also undefined, terrorism springs? Commissioner Patten recently had a high-profile dispute with the US over the 'axis of evil' and the excesses of the current war. His concerns are valid, but come very late in the day. How can we endorse the practices and structures of NATO, including its undermining of the UN and of international law, and then hope to restrain the dominant power within NATO? Too often, while we agonize over whether the ends justify the means, we discover that in endorsing the means we have pre-selected the ends (see Maguire, 2002, p. 36).

This applies also to a war on Iraq, which may have come closer – even started – by the time of reading. The dispute over whether Saddam Hussein has weapons of mass destruction – whilst terrifying – is beside the point here. Quite apart from questions of consistency, we have to ask how a major offensive against an enemy of his known ruthlessness can hope to make those weapons less of a danger to the surrounding region and beyond. We also face the disintegration of Iraq in circumstances of war, and its impact on the Kurds; this has implications for Turkish and other interventions.

An alternative is put forward by a former UN Under Secretary-General, Sir Brian Urquhart, and a seasoned US scholar and State Department adviser, William R. Polk of the University of Chicago. The latter starts by detailing why until 1990 the US 'alternative' was actually *supporting* Saddam:

> It was also the policy of the British, French, and Russian governments. All of us did it for similar reasons: we opposed the fundamentalist Shi'ite revolutionary regime of Iran; we all sought markets for our arms; we wanted Iraqi oil; and we accepted the beguiling vision of Saddam's regime as both powerful and pliant. (Polk, 1999, p. 34)

He then goes through all other alternatives, detailing the troubled UNSCOM arms-inspection saga.

> To achieve the changes we want, we must seek to ameliorate the condition of the Iraqi people and to get them back on the road to economic development . . . There is little chance of the evolution of a more open society under the shadow of search-and-destroy operations or aerial bombardment, or even under the stringency of sanctions . . . [;] by making use of economic pressures and incentives, and by basing our policies on an analysis of Iraqi and US interests, we should be able to nudge the Iraqis in this direction. (ibid.)

Sir Brian Urquhart considers other accounts and proposed remedies.

> I found myself turning once again to the quiet voice of William R. Polk . . . These goals entail diplomatic efforts

> to stabilize the situation in the Gulf, especially with regard to Iran, Saddam's most dreaded enemy; to limit arms shipments and especially the proliferation of nuclear weapons; and to embark on a long-term initiative to create a Middle Eastern zone free of weapons of mass destruction. (Urquhart, 1999a, p. 29)

To some, the fact that this was not done over the past decade makes it irrelevant and war is the answer. To the rest of us, war has been brought closer precisely by the failure to implement such an alternative. We have been told as much by two former UN humanitarian chiefs in Iraq, Dennis Halliday and Hans von Sponeck:

> What we describe is not conjecture. These are undeniable facts known to us as two former insiders . . . British and US intelligence agencies know well that Iraq is qualitatively disarmed, and they have not forgotten that the outgoing secretary of defence, William Powell, told incoming President George Bush in January: 'Iraq no longer poses a military threat to its neighbours' . . . We are horrified by the prospects of a new US-led war against Iraq. The implications of 'finishing unfinished business' in Iraq are too serious for the global community to ignore . . . What is now most urgently needed is an attack on injustice, not on the Iraqi people. (*Guardian*, 29 November 2001)

Hope Comes at Last: East Timor's Coalition of the Willing

The same year that saw the NATO war on Serbia over Kosova brought another crisis, and potential catastrophe, on the other side of the globe. East Timor had been invaded in 1975, and annexed in 1976, by Indonesia under General Suharto. That occupation introduced a regime of oppression, under Kopassus special forces. Up to 250,000 East Timorese died through massacre and famine. The East Timorese maintained a continuous struggle for independence, often ignored because, as one diplomat put it, 'Indonesia matters and East Timor doesn't' (Shawcross, 2000, p. 358). Numerous Security Council resolutions calling on Indonesia to end the annexation were not acted upon, four of the five permanent members continuing arms supply to Jakarta (Hyland, 2000, p. 58).

After economic crisis and riots toppled Suharto, his successor, B.J. Habibie, agreed to a referendum, fondly trusting the East Timorese would choose Indonesian rule. Habibie refused any foreign troop presence and the UN walked into yet another under-resourced operation, bringing only 300 unarmed civilian police to oversee the vote. It embarked on an ambitious voter education programme, but had twice to postpone the vote because Indonesia's promise of providing security, and curbing its own militia, was unsurprisingly broken. When the vote was held on 30 August 1999, 98 per cent voted, almost 80 per cent of them for independence. Though Habibie said he accepted the result, the Kopassus and the militias swung into action, whether directed from Jakarta or following their own agenda.

The world confronted a new disaster – some feared another genocide – and seemed unable or unwilling to prevent it. Prime Minister Howard was ready for Australia to lead an intervention force, if Indonesia agreed. As the various powers, and the Security Council, deliberated, people were being driven from their homes, many hacked to death, and the university in Dili – the East Timorese capital – and essential services destroyed. Nobel Prize-winner Bishop Belo had to flee to Australia, unable to protect the 2,000 people who turned to him for refuge.

Attention now focused on the UN compound in Dili, amid fears of a massacre. Kofi Annan kept regular contact with President Habibie, but could not convince him that his troops had lost control or that an international force was required. General Wiranto, the Indonesian army commander, was confronted with the scene on the ground in Dili by a Security Council mission. At that time, various countries announced a suspension of arms sales and the IMF postponed a scheduled visit. Jakarta eventually accepted the principle of UN intervention, although still haggling over its leadership.

The next day, however, 12 September, Habibie telephoned Kofi Annan to say that he accepted intervention and that it could be led by Australia. On 15 September the Security Council authorized a force, and it arrived in Dili on 20 September. Though the violence and the destruction were far from over, the basis was set from which then emerged UNTAET (United Nations Transitional Authority in East Timor), which this year handed over to an East Timorese administration after presidential elections.

It would be as difficult to overstate these momentous events, as it would be to recapture the sense of raging despair that settled over all the friends of East Timor, particularly our own East Timor Ireland Solidarity Campaign (ETISC), in the dog days of late August/early September. As the United Nations, far from engaging with the bloodbath, appeared set to disengage itself, its name seemed a byword for cowardice and cynical betrayal. The UN's dramatic about-turn – not before time, and not before tragic harm had been done – had a number of major sources.

Its central players were of course the East Timorese people themselves, whose courage and long endurance inspired others to join their struggle. One such ally was the publicly visible face of the UN, Secretary-General Kofi Annan.

> This was a significant achievement for Annan – with unprecedented speed, the Security Council had unanimously approved a Chapter VII peace enforcement intervention in a member state. (Shawcross, 2000, p. 360)

Mr Annan had indeed negotiated a diplomatic 'minefield'. He had managed this largely because of the moral and political authority which he had acquired, especially because of the open attitude to his own and the UN's past errors which he had already begun to manifest (see pp. 52 ff. above). One could argue that authorization was unnecessary, because East Timor was not Indonesian territory and/or because the Genocide Convention is sufficient in itself, but even if this is true the risks involved would have been horrendous. What matters is that authorization was given, despite, for example, China's tendency to support Indonesia on East Timor because of its own annexation of Tibet (Hyland, 2000, p. 58).

This achievement owed much to Mr Annan's personal skills and deployment of his authority. It is not for nothing that Mr Habibie made his crucial call to Mr Annan 'as a personal friend and as a friend of Indonesia' (Shawcross, op.cit., p. 360). There is even less doubt that such bridges could not have been built without some other key players, the UN volunteers of Dili. These were the civilian observers, journalists and others who simply refused to withdraw from East Timor after 8 September.

This was truly a turning-point in world history. A group of volunteers decided that they owned the United Nations and would not abandon it to the ambitions or the amnesia of the great powers. It is a cause for pride that among them were Irish observers and volunteers, standing *'sa bhearna baoil'* ('in the gap of danger'). These in turn would not have been there but for the work of Tom Hyland, founder of the ETISC, in campaigning to raise consciousness of a neglected struggle and then to bring it to fruition with the independence vote. He played a pivotal role in those days, advising and pressuring at the very highest levels.

Amidst all the conundrums and theories, these people made a living reality of the UN Charter. As Kofi Annan was to tell the world's citizens a year later:

> The Charter was written in your name . . . It is up to you
> to see the pledges honoured, and so to make the new
> century better than the old. (Annan, 2001)

These words are far from a mere token compliment; without the unofficial initiative and pressure exercised in the East Timor crisis, the UN would have gone down to yet another debilitating moral and political failure.

We can see Kosovo and East Timor, along with William Shawcross, as equally intense, but contrasting, crises for the UN.

There is a world of difference between the ways they were resolved: in Kosovo, the major powers most responsible for the weaknesses of the organization simply sidelined it during an illegal war and then made it responsible for a troubled peace; in East Timor, a bunch of stubborn civilians brought the UN, along with those same controlling powers, back to the path towards its true mandate. This is what enabled Tom Hyland, who had been in near-despair of the UN in Autumn 1999, to say in 2000:

> In my opinion the world would be a lesser place for all of us if the UN did not exist. This should not blind us however to the weak spots contained in the institution. (Hyland, 2000, p. 59)

The telling contrast with Kosovo was quietly spelt out by Mr Annan:

> He described the peacekeeping force in the former Portuguese colony as a 'coalition of the willing', armed with a security council resolution that allowed it to use 'all necessary measures' to do its job. NATO's action in Yugoslavia had no such mandate, he said. (*Guardian*, 21 September 1999)

This pinpoints an issue that comes straight home to us in Ireland. Tom Hyland pays a well-deserved tribute to Human Rights Commissioner Mary Robinson, who had made a vital intervention during August, and then to Minister for Foreign Affairs David Andrews, who had visited Dili in September 1999. Without detracting from the praise due to the Minister's courage and candour, we must note that this intervention occurred between two other actions that year which point in a much different, and more worrying, direction.

In March 1999 Mr Andrews supported EU endorsement of NATO's bombing campaign in Kosovo and later that same year he signed us into NATO/PfP (see pp. 71–73 and 81–83). One wonders for how long our governments can manage to ride the twin horses of aggressive 'peacemaking' under NATO and conflict resolution under UN auspices. When they realize that they should stop attempting this ungainly and self-defeating balancing act, will they find themselves unable to dismount from the EU/NATO warhorse?

That was Nice: Let's do it Again!

> One note that came through discussion on a fairly consistent basis was a degree of frustration that consideration be given to a 're-run' of the Nice Treaty referendum, or more specifically, to putting the 'Nice question' in the same form to people once again. (Hayes, 2002a, p. 9)

Whoever said that in life there are no dress rehearsals was not in Ireland in June 2001. Because we got the answer wrong, it turns out that that was only the pre-ferendum, with the real re-ferendum still to come. 'Referendum' means that something is brought to the people; it seems, however, that we didn't quite get it!

The government's option for 'information' without re-negotiation is telling: could we not have an adequate grasp of a document such as the Nice Treaty and still disagree with it (see John Murray SC, *The Irish Times* 6 May 2002)? This is a timely lesson in how EU democracy works when it gets down to the *demos*, and in how our political establishment prioritizes democratic process in comparison with its embarrassment vis-à-vis its fellow EU élites.

We have traced the evolution of EU military policy, and Ireland's relation to it. That evolution has continued with the Nice Treaty, on which a second referendum is planned for Autumn 2002. Some suggest that the whole Nice agenda should be transferred to the Convention on the Future of Europe, preparing the 2004 summit and a more ambitious treaty. On either scenario, it is appropriate for us to take stock of where Nice would lead us, specifically in military matters and also more generally.

Nice and a European Army?

In May 2001 we were told that it was 'unfortunate' that people thought Nice had anything to do with armies (Daniel Keohane, *The Irish Times*, 12 May 2001); unfortunate perhaps, but not unfounded. The treaty alters the existing EU Political Committee to a 'Political and Security Committee', which will exercise 'the political control and strategic direction of crisis management operations' (Ireland, 2001, p. 63). The 'Presidency Report' prepared by France for the Nice Summit, and attached to the Treaty, spells out the bodies that will implement this committee's decisions: the Military Committee, and the Military Staff, of the EU (EU, 2000, p. 3). There is also provision for special representatives on crisis situations to be appointed by majority, rather than unanimously (Bonde, 2001, p. 47).

Clearly, European common policy is being forwarded here – one of the reasons the Attorney General gave for our needing a referendum (National Platform, 2002, p. 3). Nice is anyhow a stage in developing an integrated European Union, which has declared its 'defence identity' fundamental to its presence in the world. Not only are all citizens entitled to have all aspects of that process in mind when occasionally given a voice on it; the citizens of Ireland have two particular reasons for doing so with Nice.

First, there are the Petersberg Tasks, incorporated in the Amsterdam Treaty. No sooner was that treaty ratified than there came the Kosovo intervention, NATO's rudely practical interpretation of 'peacemaking'. Minister Brian Cowen recently said: 'Concepts are fine. I'd like to see how it is envisaged in a practical way' (*The Irish Times*, 9 February 2002). Nice is our first opportunity to respond in this realistic spirit to the actuality, rather than the fine theory, of 'peacemaking'.

Second, all this arises in the context that our government frog-marched us into NATO's 'Partnership for Peace' in flagrant violation of the solemn commitment to hold a referendum. Thus we need to scrutinize what Petersberg really involves in the knowledge that we cannot rely on the political promises administered to sugar NATO/PfP and other such pills; all the more necessary, as the Presidency Report affirms a 'genuine strategic partnership', a 'permanent and effective . . . [and] trusting relationship between the EU and NATO' (EU, 2000, pp. 1, 3 and 4).

Keatinge and Tonra claim the ERRF project is 'modest', 'experimental' and 'laborious', so does not presage 'a Brave New Superstate' (Keatinge and Tonra, 2002, pp. 16, 17); yet later on it becomes 'a core EU activity' (p. 23). We have already noted the EU's self-description as 'a power, resolutely doing battle' (EU, 2001, p. 78; see p. 33 above). Our own government's White Paper on defence speaks blithely of 'the development of European military forces' (Ireland, 2000, 3.2.7). This all sounds very like, if not a single, then a multiple European army. When is an army not an army? When it's being incubated by the EU. Maybe Mr Prodi was right: 'If you don't want to call it a European army, don't call it a European army. You can call it "Margaret", you can call it "Mary-Anne", you can find any name' (*The Independent*, 4 February 2000).

One name that comes to mind is the Western European Union. Whereas Maastricht had declared it 'an integral part of the development of the Union', Nice drops all but one reference to it. This is because the EU itself has taken on the WEU's Petersberg capacities (Ireland, 2001, p. 63). Our government reassure us that this is not the integration of the WEU mooted by Amsterdam on which Ireland had noted a 'continuing lack of agreement' (Ireland, 1998, p. 118). Things are not quite so simple, however:

> The WEU Parliamentary Assembly (composed of national parliamentarians) now styles itself the interim European Security and Defence Assembly, but it is not yet clear how this squares with the role of the directly elected European Parliament in the scrutiny of the European Security and Defence Policy. (Keatinge and Tonra, 2002, p. 15)

They haven't gone away, you know!

Reassurance wears even thinner as we turn to what precisely our troops would be doing. The list is that of the Petersberg Tasks: 'humanitarian and rescue', 'peacekeeping' and 'tasks of combat forces in crisis management, including peacemaking' (ibid., p. 9). As we noted in discussing NATO/PfP, these terms are extremely vague, but include some very disquieting contents: Tony Blair called Kosovo 'humanitarian', whereas for Daniel Keohane it was 'peacemaking' (see p. 74 above). John Bruton himself has observed of peacemaking: 'It is very difficult to distinguish that from war making . . .' (Storey, 2001, p. 5).

Not only are the tasks unclear; the list is open-ended. The EU treaties – including Nice – tell us that questions covered by its policy 'shall include' the Petersberg Tasks, much as NATO/PfP's list has 'others as may subsequently be agreed' (see p. 72 above). Who decides what is in and out of these categories, and what might be added? Such vagueness would hardly pass muster in a piece of domestic legislation, which always starts with the definition of terms. This is no pedantry: the lives of many people can be affected by the precise meaning of a legal term.

Why should we tolerate such fuzzy language where it could literally mean life or death for thousands? It also has implications for our defence forces, who may be committed to operations, under such vague rubrics, which could later be the subject of prosecution at the International Criminal Court or elsewhere. When Keatinge and Tonra mention ERRF 'peacemaking', they add, 'as provided for under Chapter VII of the UN Charter' (ibid., p. 9). This is highly misleading because the ERRF is not subjected to that Charter, any more indeed than is NATO/PfP.

Of course the EU Treaty, as enacted at Maastricht and after, 'acknowledges the principles of the UN Charter', and the UN's primary role is 'frequently referred to in [EU policy] documentation' (ibid., p. 13) – how very fine and large of them! Much is made of the fact that Ireland and Sweden have specified a UN mandate for any operations they engage in, as well they might.

But this makes it clear that Ireland never bothered to insist that a UN mandate be made the cornerstone of EU policy *as such* – or else tried and failed, which would be even worse.

This is all the more worrying as both NATO and the Western European Union continue to see nuclear weapons as central to their 'defence' doctrines. How can we have a common policy on 'all questions relating to the security of the Union' with countries the majority of which are wedded to both NATO and the WEU, and yet claim that we are serious about opposition to, and elimination of, nuclear weapons? This is no mere abstract issue, as the US, at the heart of NATO, contemplates lowering the nuclear threshold. William M. Arkin of Johns Hopkins University has concluded:

> In recent months, when Bush administration officials talked about the implications of September 11 for long-term military policy, they have often focused on 'homeland defence' and the need for an anti-missile shield. In truth, what has evolved since last year's terror attacks is an integrated, significantly expanded planning doctrine for nuclear wars. (Arkin, 2002, p. 55)

We have already seen the Brahimi Report spell out how European developments have depleted UN peacekeeping capacity (p. 55 above). This is particularly significant, as Minister Cowen emphasized at our National Forum on Europe that Brahimi was unanimously endorsed by the UN General Assembly (Cowen, 2002, p. 56). Keatinge and Tonra recycle the cliché that 'current doctrine' in the UN and the EU makes Chapter VIII regional actions 'more relevant' than actions by the UN itself. Why so?

> Chapter VII of the UN Charter includes the formal obligation for all members to provide military support to the enforcement of a Security Council resolution, though in practice this provision has not been fully implemented. (p. 13)

So it is not done – because it has not been done; never mind that it is a solemn obligation to the allegedly 'primary' UN!

Why are EU members not making a reality of Article 47 of the UN Charter, providing for a 'Military Committee' all right – but that of the UN itself? This becomes poignantly ironic when we realize that the 'modest, experimental' ERRF – a mere salami-slice off the EU's potential capacity, we might say – involves a rotation from some 200,000 personnel (see Lewis, 2000, p. 1). This compares to the Brahimi Report's figure of 147,900 pledged from 87 member states to the UN Standby Arrangements System for the entire world (UN, 2000, para. 102). The UN Department of Peacekeeping Operations informed me in June 2002 that there had not been a significant increase in pledges to UNSAS, and that the total of member states involved was now 74. Well may Keatinge and Tonra call the ERRF 'similar' to these UN arrangements (ibid., p. 12); read it and weep.

In the very same week as the government devised their wording for the re-ferendum, the Minister for Defence announced certain operational decisions about UN peacekeeping:

> Ireland is also due to end its involvement in Eritrea next year. Mr. Smith said it has become more difficult over the years to recruit for missions on a regular basis, and to meet necessary mandates. The Defence Forces will [be] continuing [their] training programme at home, meanwhile, in preparation for the commitment to make 850 troops available to the European rapid reaction force. (*Irish Independent*, 26 June 2002)

Keatinge and Tonra selectively quote the clause about the defence policy of 'certain member states', omitting the explicit reference to NATO (pp. 21-22; see pp. 66–70 above). They see this as 'allowing for' policies like ours, revealing that the main thrust of the EU policy is clearly something else. They stress that the force levels involved are relatively small compared to EU members' own troop levels. The problem with these protestations of modesty is that they are all too often tinged with regret.

This emerges, for example, in 'an awareness of over-dependence on the United States'(p. 7).

There is one clear way to address such dependence, while avoiding the perception of becoming a competitor in the superpower stakes, and that is to strengthen the UN. Nobody is better placed to make an effective reality of the UN Charter than the various well-off European countries, including Ireland. The demonstration effect of placing their already enormous military and other resources at the effective disposal of that body would arguably be the greatest practical step anyone could make today for world peace.

This has a direct bearing on our topic, and on a forthcoming referendum, since proponents of the EU military structures make great play of their importance as a corrective to US military predominance: Europe, we are told, needs more 'clout', to 'punch its weight'. If this means that the EU hopes to act as a moderating influence, it is a strange way of going about it, and the results and prospects to date are far from encouraging. If it means that the EU envisages competing with the US in military strength, things look even worse. On either scenario, the EU would have forgone a unique opportunity to affirm a revitalized UN as the cornerstone of an urgently necessary regime of effective peace building and international law (see pp. 97–99 above).

Keatinge and Tonra admit that 'the ERRF may reasonably be described as a form of militarisation' (p. 16). They tell us, however, that NATO's use of air power in Bosnia and Kosovo is not evidence of militarism 'when the whole experience of conflict in the Balkans in the 1990s is taken into account' (ibid.). The point of genuine peace building, however, in any of its forms is to change, not to absorb and reflect, the context of conflict.

They present our choices as between 'opt-out' (bad) and 'watchful engagement' (good). They give four reasons against 'opt-out'. The first is that if we are in the ERRF we can have an influence on what it does. This might be more reassuring if we had ever shown signs of wanting, let alone having such influence on policy so far, and it does raise the question of where we draw the line: should the Garda become a member of organized crime so as to direct its future activities to better ends?

They then dismiss the (clearly naïve) idea that the UN/OSCE is a preferable framework. They say more than they mean to when they tell us it is 'no accident' that current missions in Bosnia and Kosovo 'operate in the NATO framework, within which the United States is the leading element' (ibid., p. 7). It is indeed no accident, but the result of that systematic undermining, sidelining and subordination of the UN which we have already recounted. Of course, we are told, the UN and its associated OSCE are a 'good thing':

> It has to be borne in mind, however, that these organisations – while necessary and complementary bases for the state's overall security policy – are not the forum in which the evolution of the Rapid Reaction Force will be decided. (ibid., p. 24)

This pure tautology means that our most solemn international obligations, though 'necessary', are now merely 'complementary' to the real business of security – and they still say there is no strain within Irish foreign policy?

Thirdly, not being in would leave us in 'mute denial' (presumably inferior to mute acquiescence, as over Kosovo) whenever the ERRF was deployed. This is hugely significant: we are told we would be able to join in nothing if not in the club. Why so? It must mean that ERRF membership would significantly reconfigure our defence forces, with serious implications for UN peacekeeping, for which the same 850 troops are 'double-hatted' (perhaps a wise precaution in all this muddle!).

Why is it that we can decide cases on their merits inside, but not outside, the ERRF and NATO/PfP? Maybe the defence analyst Jonathan Eyal was right to caution us that long lead-times and procurement commitments would make it in practice almost impossible to withdraw at the last moment, as we are constantly told we could do (see Storey, 2001, pp. 4–5). Otherwise, if good work, from disaster relief to UN-authorized peace enforcement, is being done, why couldn't we co-operate then and there?

The fourth reason why we have to be 'in' is that poor oul' cliché, that it 'would diminish Irish influence' within the EU policy. So a fully fledged EU member, demonstrably committed to an active peacekeeping role under the UN, cannot have adequate influence within EU policy unless signed up to a military structure the leading members of which have aligned it with NATO but refused to subordinate it explicitly to the UN's authority. There is indeed a serious problem, but just whose problem is it?

These four reasons are variations on a single obsessive theme: if we don't agree with things, people might think we don't agree with things. There is one forbidden word in Ireland's EU lexicon – the word No. Our élite are not used to saying it and the outlook for improvement is poor since they proved unable even to *hear* it in June 2001. In the re-ferendum campaign our case will be called irresponsible, self-indulgent, and the rest, but it is not an argument for uninvolvement. It is an argument for engaging in a realistic critical dialogue with our EU neighbours, while honouring, and implementing in practice, our fundamental commitment to the full spectrum of UN-directed peacekeeping.

We Don't Heed no Declaration: We Demand a Protocol!

In June 2001 the Irish electorate sent back the salade Niçoise. Headwaiter Bertie, and his assistants, were too afraid of Chef Romano and the catering committee to report this setback. After sulking a while in the pantry, they decided they'd wait a little and then serve it up again, without altering the recipe. At the same time, they announced that nothing else was on the menu, and if we didn't eat it up there'd be no more dinners ever again. When some of us – quite unreasonably – pointed out that it was now wilted and even less palatable than before, they graciously promised that next time it would be served on a beautiful new plate, with embossed declarations around the edge.

Much will be made, in the re-ferendum, of two solemn

Declarations about the Nice Treaty which were issued, one by the European Council, and the other by the Irish government, at the Seville EU summit of June 2002 (see *The Irish Times*, 22 June 2002). We were immediately told that this pair of Declarations put an end to any debate or discussion about military concerns in relation to Nice: the question had been taken off the agenda. There are serious reasons to query this diktat.

The first problem is that declarations are, by their very definition, not part of the binding text of a treaty, but are opinions, promises and the like – however solemnly worded and delivered – about that text. They do not have legal force over the EU collectively, and on Ireland's part they amount only to a political promise, not a legal commitment. They have been made precisely and only because our government have ignored the electorate's concerns about the treaty text, opting instead to din us into silence by loudly insisting that we do not understand it. It is as if an insurance salesperson, when we raise some point about the small print, whipped the policy out of our hands, saying: 'Never mind that – look at this list of satisfied customers!'

The central argument of this essay has been that there is a growing tension between our proclaimed foreign policy values and what we are now involved in under the common EU policy. The Government's triumphant brandishing of not one but two distinct declarations dramatically focuses this tension. Most tellingly, the Irish declaration starts by referring to the primacy of the United Nations, whereas the EU declaration makes no mention of the UN at all. Elsewhere, the tension is disguised by omission, for example where both declarations selectively quote the article about the character of certain member states' policies, but neither completes the sentence, which specifically requires EU policy – to which we are committed – to be compatible with that of NATO (see pp. 66–70 and 111 above).

The government claim that these declarations remove all doubt about a threat to our neutrality, but that in deference to their opponents they have even gone a step further. The wording for the re-ferendum will contain an added sentence which, we are told, safeguards Ireland against any future EU decision to have a 'common defence'; we could not take on an EU common defence obligation without a further referendum (see *The Irish Times*, 28 June 2002). It is far from clear that this adds anything not already implied by the Supreme Court decision in the Crotty case (see pp. 67–8 above), or that it would indeed allow Ireland to approve a common defence whilst remaining outside it, along the lines of the Danish protocol. More important for our present purposes, it does not deal with the problems raised by the Nice Treaty as such.

The government have made much of the role of the National Forum on Europe, and of how their various wordings have been derived from the Forum process. Here again however they have re-enacted precisely the top-down, 'we know what you really need' attitude that they profess to have outgrown. They chose not to circulate proposals for the two declarations, or for the referendum wording, at the Forum to get people's responses. If they regard such a consultative process as out of the question, they really have failed to get the message about democratic process.

Instead of consulting us, they simply tell us that their various wordings take care of all our concerns. This is implausible. The Forum's chairperson, for example, spelt out three distinct questions arising from its work in this area: first, the contents and implications of Nice and previous treaties; second, the question of a future defence guarantee, and third, the conditions under which we participate in peacekeeping and conflict prevention (Hayes, 2002b, pp. 37–38). It is striking that only on the second of these three questions – the *possibility* of a common defence guarantee *in the future* – have the government offered a specific constitutional commitment.

That proposed constitutional commitment fails to address the urgent need for an effective government assurance that:

> nothing it commits to under Nice, or indeed earlier treaties, requires, suggests, or implies a departure from

Ireland's traditional policy of military neutrality or the values underlying it. (Hayes 2002b, p. 37).

Our present concerns are with the text of the Nice Treaty, as the latest stage of cumulative EU policy developments, and with the situation in which these now land us. The government claim to have addressed those concerns, but it is ludicrous to respond to them with mere declarations to the effect that the treaty has no impact on the orientation of Irish defence policy. Either our participation in the European Rapid Reaction Force, the Political and Security Committee, the Military Committee and the Military Staff of the EU undermines our approach to foreign and defence policy or it does not; no tacked-on formula of words can alter that.

Here we must briefly address the issue of confusion, which the government has blamed on those who question their policies. It is of course possible that all the fuss over Nice is the product of naïveté, or worse, on the part of its opponents. It is however equally likely that the alleged 'confusion' represents the belated arrival into the daylight of matters which successive governments have preferred to obscure for the past fifteen years or more. In the debates over the Single European Act, Maastricht and Amsterdam, the establishment blandly insisted that any concerns about military matters were at best futuristic scaremongering; nothing significant was happening right now, and anything significant would be up for decision in the future (see p. 66 above).

Now we are loftily informed that, as regards the Rapid Reaction Force, it has all been decided far in the past! The consent obtained from the electorate to the Maastricht and Amsterdam treaties, where the entire establishment assured them there was nothing disturbing at stake, turns out to have committed us, we are now told, to significant common military policies in the shape of the ERRF. Mr. John Bruton had the gall to declare, on RTE radio news on 25 June 2002, that 'people may not have realized that' when voting on the Maastricht and Amsterdam treaties. Well might people 'not have realized' it: the entire establishment were blue in the face assuring them that it was not so.

Whatever about a common defence, we seem to be already up to our necks in a common European offence. The situation would be quite different with a Protocol, within the text, such as the Danes negotiated at Amsterdam:

> With regard to measures adopted by the Council in the fields of Articles J.3(1) and J.7 of the [Amsterdam Treaty], Denmark does not participate in the elaboration and the implementation of decisions and actions of the Union which have defence implications, but will not prevent the development of closer cooperation between member states in this area. Therefore Denmark shall not participate in their adoption. Denmark shall not be obliged to contribute to the financing of the operational expenditure arising from such measures. (Storey, 2001, p. 20)

Denmark was able to act on its perceived interests, and our government presumably have not even tried to do so; if they tried and were prevented, then their reassurances to us are clearly set at nought. The Danes at least have done us some service in driving a wedge between EU membership as such and an automatic obligation to take part in the ERRF.

Such a protocol is the minimum necessary to allow us to retrieve and restore our commitment to the priority of peaceful conflict resolution under the UN. It would be far preferable if all our EU colleagues embraced the same commitment – with truly electrifying effects on the present troubled state of world conflict. If, however, they remain adamant, we can do no good by pretending to agree with them. In a world of epidemic warfare, where most victims are perforce silent even after the guns cease firing, we have a duty to raise our voice and outgrow our fantasies of peer pressure.

One of the central merits claimed for the Irish declaration is that it solemnizes the 'triple-lock' mechanism which, the government says, protects us from pressure to join in any repugnant military action: UN authorization, government decision and Dáil approval (see *The Irish Times*, 22 June 2002). We are assured that no commitment of troops overseas will take place without the fulfilment of all these three conditions. Again, our experience to date raises a number of difficulties with these assurances.

At first sight, they seem merely to restate a fundamental principle, Article 28.3.1 of our Constitution, which requires that:

> War shall not be declared and the State shall not participate in any war save with the assent of Dáil Éireann. (Ireland, 1999b, p. 96)

The Constitution gives the key to the Irish people, because only they can agree to remove this requirement of Dáil assent to actual war. The 'triple lock', however, is something quite else: a set of procedures – part legal, part political – which are not protected by the Constitution and yet would apply to military operations including combat.

The overseas operations envisaged under the 'triple lock' mechanism are not regarded by our establishment politicians as acts of war, however near they come to them; Mr. John Bruton's observations on the difficulty of distinguishing 'peacemaking' from actual warfare are the nearest they have come to clarity on that point (see p. 109 above). If anything indeed, our governments have tended to under- rather than over-interpret Article 28.3.1, as when they have recently claimed a direct prerogative to grant landing rights for warplanes at Shannon, claiming that this was not actual participation in a war. Such a claim, it should be noted, is not affected by the Irish declaration; which deals only with actual commitment of Irish troops.

The suggestion that the Irish people should rely on the 'triple lock' in relation to the EU's Rapid Reaction Force is in itself an erosion of a vital constitutional principle: it gives our politicians a key to combat, with no guarantee that we can get it back. Still worse: any government of the day possesses the screwdriver that could dismantle the whole mechanism without reference back to us, the householder. A simple government majority could 'streamline' the Defence Act to remove the requirements of UN sanction and/or Dáil approval for what by that stage would be presented as mere 'routine' ERRF operations. The consensus between our major establishment parties on such matters would make this all the easier.

When this argument is dismissed as intellectually dishonest scaremongering, we might recall that we are not dealing with merely abstract scenarios far in the future. The previous government, under the present Taoiseach, quite brazenly did something far worse than the prospect just considered: the broken promise on NATO/PfP was about a *referendum*, something even more fundamental than a vote of Dáil Éireann. This marks our cards for us: any commitment in this area will be subjected to later legal scrutiny to see how it can be circumvented. We have reason to be wary about any mere political promise, especially in this specific policy area, after our experience with the non-ferendum on NATO/PfP.

Any government that can blithely offer a Dáil vote in place of a promised referendum would have little hesitation about installing a cabinet decision in place of a Dáil vote. This latter has indeed happened in relation to landing rights for other countries' warplanes at Shannon. During the Gulf War of 1991, there was a Dáil debate over the decision, whereas in the case of warplanes headed for Afghanistan in 2001 the government simply claimed a prerogative. We must also be wary lest a similar erosion should affect the seemingly straightforward notion of 'authorization of the operation' by the UN (*The Irish Times*, 22 June 2002), particularly as this is a requirement only at the political level rather than a constitutional guarantee.

Nor can we be reassured by the prospects for Irish government participation at the EU level of decision-making. Admittedly, majority voting is excluded where decisions have 'military or defence implications' (Ireland, 1997, p. 114), but this leaves us with two problems. Not only are the distinctions between military/defence and other implications somewhat hazy at best; who in any case can foresee, when agreeing a policy position, what precise implications it will turn out to have down the road? This is crucial, because common positions not having defence or military implications, as well as the actual implementation of positions already adopted, are agreed by majority vote rather than unanimity.

There is of course provision for an 'emergency brake' procedure, which can refer a majority-vote question back to the European Council, if a government invokes 'important and stated reasons of national policy' (Ireland, 1997, p. 114). Not only is this, as its nickname implies, designed and regarded as exceptional; it also returns the matter to the very forum where our governments walked us into all these tangles in the first place. It is hard to envisage an Irish government, having been unprepared to state a principled objection to a whole tranche of policies as they evolved, subsequently objecting to their implementation under the circumstances of an actual crisis and all the pressures it would bring.

We may recall that this is no mere hypothetical forecast: the Irish government acquiesced in the EU endorsement of NATO's Kosovo bombardment (see pp. 81–82 above). If they point out – as was their wont over Afghanistan and Shannon more recently – that this is different from actually doing the bombing, who then are the hypocrites? We have thus as much reason to abhor what our governments have already accepted as to distrust their promises to reject the unacceptable in the future.

These governments, moreover, constantly warn us of the dangers of being perceived as 'unhelpful' or 'anti-European' on any issue, let alone that of war and peace. Does the reaction of our political establishment to the rejection of the Nice Treaty give any basis at all for believing them that – whoever is in government – they will exercise their much-trumpeted right, in the hour of crisis, not to go along with unacceptable military action? If so, why on earth did they endorse Kosovo?

Nice, Peace and Democracy: an Unlikely Trio?

> It would be constitutionally suspect and an arrogant and undemocratic rejection of the will of the people if ratification of an unrevised Treaty was pursued. (Former Attorney-General John Rogers SC, *The Irish Times*, 6 May 2002).

Keatinge and Tonra cite poll findings that 12 per cent said concern about neutrality influenced their No vote, which was 'a long way behind the issue of the decision-making process' (op. cit., p. 4). This essay has, however, argued that questions of defence cannot be divorced from questions of democratic decision-making. Our lack of information and control on war-making is merely the worst instance of our lack of information and control on society in general and its direction. Those concerned with decision-making have much cause for concern about defence and *vice versa*.

Some readers may agree with the case made here, but yet believe, reluctantly, that they still must vote for Nice because the overall benefits are so great or the implications of rejection so awful. The Treaty has been presented as containing changes that are both necessary and good, without which Europe would face disaster. We need briefly to consider these claims, as people ponder their vote in a second referendum.

Those last words provide part of the answer: what kind of Euro-democracy is being built by the insistence that we keep voting until we get the right answer? It is a moral certainty that a lower Yes margin, on a lower turnout, would have been snapped up as a done deal. 'Informed public debate' on the EU is clearly a one-way street; it's not that you vote, but what you vote, that matters. Will the Yes side in a new referendum agree to a third vote if the margin is again as low?

But maybe this indecent haste is for a good reason – the task of EU enlargement? There is in fact a remarkable consensus on enlargement:

> All participating parties and groups have indicated that they support enlargement – no voice opposed to the process has been raised. (Hayes, 2002a, p. 8)

Can this be achieved without Nice? The Commission President thinks so:

> Legally, ratification of the Nice Treaty is not necessary for enlargement. It's without any problem up to 20 members, and those beyond 20 members have only to put in the accession agreement some notes of change, some clause. But legally, it's not necessary . . . [;] from this specific point of view, enlargement is possible without Nice. (Romano Prodi, *The Irish Times*, 21 June 2001)

The prompt re-bagging of that particular cat indicates that enlargement is in fact being deployed not for its intrinsic merits but manipulatively, to ensure that the Nice package is not re-opened – again, hardly an excessively democratic procedure.

But maybe there is something else so vital in Nice that we ought to grin and bear it? One basic provision is 'enhanced co-operation', the right of a group of members to set up systems in which the rest are not involved. Under Amsterdam, all EU members, even if not included, had to agree, for example on the Euro. Under Nice, a majority can set up such systems, even if others are opposed. No harm in that, you might say, if progress would otherwise be stymied; but what price democratic dialogue, the basic requirement of carrying our fellow-citizens with us?

Such concerns reach far beyond the stubborn nationalist camp. It is no longer possible to claim that Nice reflects the progressive consensus and its opponents are merely backward. Two experts from the very heart of the EU project itself have warned us that the removal by Nice of the right of each country to a Commissioner was, 'perhaps, the least considered and most unwise provision, in relation to its importance and its consequences, that has ever been written into an EU Treaty' (Gallagher and Temple Lang, 2002, p. 12).

> We believe that . . . a Commission that is not fully representative of the Union . . . is a diminished body in every sense . . . The major Member States have wanted to diminish the Commission from the beginning . . . If the EU goes the way some countries want, it won't exist in the future. (Gallagher, 2002, pp. 26, 31, 33)

This warning comes from John Temple Lang of TCD and Oxford University, an expert on EU law, and Eamonn Gallagher, former Director-General at the Commission. These are no stubborn 'anti-Europeans', but enthusiasts, otherwise pro-Nice, who are seriously concerned lest the plans of larger countries should distort, even destroy, the EU itself.

Those of us who are particularly concerned about EU military policy may connect this warning about balance between the Commission and the member states to the Commission's recent proposals to the Convention on the Future of Europe. Introducing those proposals, Mr. Prodi sailed blithely beyond what has been proposed, but not yet ratified, in Nice. It is envisaged that the Commission would take on the leading role in foreign policy, including ERRF military operations.

> 'In this context, it has to be said that the formula in the Treaty of Nice whereby it is up to the Political and Security Committee, which will soon have some thirty members, to ensure political control and strategic direction of crisis-management operations under the responsibility of the council, remains unsatisfactory', the submission states . . . [I]t makes clear that the EU's four neutral member-states should not have a veto on military or foreign policy action . . . 'This means not scaling down to accommodate the reticence of some, but seeking credibility and effectiveness through a policy which sets out to safeguard, outside the Union's own borders, certain values which are essential to our democracies. *Unanimity in foreign policy for the enlarged Union is no more relevant than it is in trade*,' the document states. (Dennis Staunton, *The Irish Times*, 23 May 2002; my emphasis.)

Our government might claim that they do not share this last, shocking suggestion. It is however dispiriting that in the Nice negotiations they were prepared to 'go to the wall' to preserve a veto over taxation, whilst apparently unperturbed by intensified EU militarization.

Many believe that anything at all that shifts the focus from the nation state towards a larger union is good, as it will enlarge horizons and diminish tensions. But those actually driving the process are fuelled largely by that mixture of democratic rhetoric and élitist practice which we have earlier encountered (see pp. 25–31 above). Rather than transcending the nation state for a greater democracy, they sense that their style of top-down politics will find more fulfilment in a larger and remoter arena: élite shall speak unto élite, and it shall be called democracy.

Those who truly want a larger democracy, rather than merely a larger union calling itself democratic, should pay heed to the unfinished business of democracy in our existing societies, as well as in the union between them. Trivializing our democratic decision procedures is scarcely an encouraging start.

A number of participants in the EU's Convention have even suggested that Nice could be quietly ignored, and its questions better addressed at the 2004 summit. It would be an agonizing dilemma if our arguments on EU military policy had to be discounted in favour of an otherwise excellent and indispensable Nice Treaty. A kind providence has saved us from any such dilemma.

Restating Neutrality: Building a Safer World

This essay has contested the official version, that our defence policy within the EU has maintained and enhanced our established values. It has argued that there is a conflict between what we are getting involved in now and our adherence to conflict resolution under the UN. This is because those with whom we have gone along have deliberately crafted a 'zero-sum' competition between the UN and themselves to the point where we can no longer pretend that the two lines of policy are compatible.

We are told there is consensus because neutrality is 'a policy espoused by successive Irish Governments'. However, this is qualified as 'military neutrality', whose 'core defining characteristic is non-membership of military alliances' (Ireland, 1999a, p. 7). It is totally inadequate to narrow the defence issue to formal membership of alliances, and that in turn to the question of mutual defence commitments. Our defence policy has already been reshaped by EU structures displaying many of the characteristics of aggressive great-power policy which were among our reasons for non-alignment in earlier decades.

When governments say that neutrality is not 'doctrinaire . . . frozen in time and isolated' (ibid.), they are unconvincing because they themselves so often caricature it as just such a fossil, lest its vitality have any real impact. It is not credible to claim that the values and principles guiding Irish foreign policy in the postwar years, and through our first decades in the UN, are still reflected in the policies and structures whose evolution this essay has traced. We owe it to ourselves and our neighbours to reclaim those values and principles.

The central significance of neutrality in 1939 was that Ireland retained its capacity to decide; choice and debate were really possible. Subsequent policy was that of a recently independent society with a sense of its distinctness from the great military powers. The leader who articulated neutrality also spoke strongly for our entry into the UN because this fulfilled our peace-oriented foreign policy. It was shameful of the last government to quote, in support of involvement with NATO, Eamon de Valera's argument in support of entry to the UN:

> the representations which you might have been able to make successfully within will not be at all possible without. (Ireland, 1999a, p. 9)

De Valera argued for the UN as all-inclusive, subordinating military force to international law and human needs. This approach could now guide the reassertion of our foreign policy values, but not because we want to be uninvolved or to look down on the rest of the world. What remains of our democratically controlled defence policy is – though imperfect – less dangerous to Europe and the world than what the EU and NATO are creating. We owe it to ourselves and others not to abandon, but to redouble, our opposition to militarism.

It is a commonplace to invoke our proud peacekeeping record with the UN, but less common to look closely at what that record is and how it was sustained. We were regarded as one of the few countries who could be genuine honest brokers in crisis situations. This gave us a role unavailable to more powerful countries, who were immediately seen as interested players in the situation and/or identified with one side in the Cold War. The White Paper on foreign policy pointed out that by 1996 Irish soldiers had served over 42,000 tours of duty as peacekeepers, and 75 had died on active service (Ireland, 1996, p. 194). The Department of Defence reports that the total number of 'tours of duty' has now risen to 50,000 and the number of deaths to 84.

We also had a peacekeeping style which built from the ground up, respecting and working through local conditions, for example in the Lebanon. This contrasted with the more top-down and aggressive style of other countries (which has disturbingly permeated our recent recruitment advertising). It has been our particular asset and it has been highly valued in various crisis situations. We have not adequately grasped this as a society, nor done sufficient honour to our fellow-citizens who have served and even given their lives, in disproportionate numbers, as peacekeeping troops.

If genuinely defensive force is sometimes required, we should be grateful that some of our fellow-citizens undertake the life of the soldier. We should enable them to perform a professional role by establishing relevant contemporary objectives and supplying the means to fulfil them. This does not require – indeed it is incompatible with – accommodation to a 'security architecture' which has so damagingly confused issues of peacekeeping, human rights and humanitarian action with aggressive militarism, including the nuclear 'first strike'.

But can our opposition to current trends amount to more than noble words from the sidelines; what in practice could we *do*? We lay claim to an enterprise culture, though suspecting that our enterprise has been more in getting wealth from elsewhere than in creating it ourselves. Be that as it may, we are (although internally very unequal) by any standards now a wealthy society; perhaps it is time for some real enterprise. Real entrepreneurs do not scan the market nervously, but actively alter their environment. We have all the resources to speak truth to our friends and neighbours and help make an active difference by making the world safer for others and ourselves.

There is at least one clear practical course we could take. Why not, for example, recall the clear message of the Brahimi Report, that richer countries have walked away from direct UN peacekeeping and that European developments have depleted the personnel available to the UN (p. 55 above)? Why not connect that with the proposal by former Under Secretary-General Sir Brian Urquhart for a 'UN Volunteer Military Force' (Urquhart, 1993), and with the fact that even the framework for a UN response capacity has not yet been properly developed? Why not dedicate the troops, currently 'double-hatted' between the UN and EU, directly to such a UN structure?

How could our EU colleagues, who profess the primacy of the UN, and constantly invoke pluralism and diversity, object to our contributing in this way? Cannot we lessen dependence on the US in a way that does not risk building an alternative superpower in Europe, whose vast military capacities are small only relative to those of the US? With the Rapid Reaction Force preparing to operate up to 4,000 km from Brussels, who will otherwise reassure non-European countries that they are not confronting 'the white race in arms' (Martin Walker, *Guardian*, 27 October 1998)?

Our troops would find there was plenty to do, as is clear from the UN reports we have considered. They could undertake inventive work in all dimensions from peace-building doctrine through logistics and communications to technological innovation and application. We could make the same *kind* of contribution for which we have previously been respected, and indeed we could do much more. We are not uniquely wonderful, but we are in a uniquely challenging place and time. If we need new resources, military or other, to do so, we can develop or acquire those resources. If others try to deprive us of knowledge or resources vital to peacekeeping, just because we have not signed up with them, then we should be wary of the 'partnership' they are talking about.

The real partnership for peace is that of societies which use their abilities and their resources to work peacefully together, and, when conflicts cannot be prevented, try to resolve them under international law through the United Nations. We have achieved a lot for ourselves and have made a contribution, of which we can be proud, to that real partnership. We can make a creative difference if we practice, and urge on our European colleagues, a more inclusive and less aggressive approach to world security. This would involve a creative posing of questions such as:

- what are the technical and moral criteria for non-offensive defence?
- how can weapons production be reduced and reshaped along non-offensive defence lines?
- what is the best practice available for conversion from military to civilian production?
- how best can conflict-prevention and conflict-resolution skills be developed and disseminated?

The practical and policy suggestions made in these final pages are consistent with the values we have preached and practised since we joined the United Nations. Those values and their practice have come under increasing strain in the past 15 years or so.

The source of that strain has been eloquently depicted by US General Lee Butler, with disquieting echoes from our recent experience and an urgent warning as to where our current drift may take us.

> The cold light of dispassionate scrutiny was shuttered in the name of security, doubts dismissed in the name of an acute and unrelenting threat, objections overruled by the incantations of the nuclear priesthood. The penalties proved to be severe. Vitally important decisions were routinely taken without adequate understanding, assertions too often prevailed over analysis, requirements took on organizational biases, technological opportunity and corporate profit drove force levels and capability, and political opportunism intruded on calculations of military necessity. (Butler, 1999, p. 10)

We have a choice.

Bibliography

Adams, Nassau 1994: 'The UN's Neglected Brief – "The Advancement of All Peoples"?', in Childers, ed., pp. 26–50.

Afri (Action from Ireland) 1996: *Links: Ireland's Links with the Arms Trade and Military Industry* (Dublin). www.afri.buz.org

Afri 1999a: *Should Ireland Join Nato's Partnership for Peace?* (Dublin).

Afri 1999b: *What Price Peace? The Irish Peace Process and the International Arms Trade* (Dublin).

Amnesty International 2000: *Ireland and the Arms Trade – Decoding the Deals* (Dublin).

Amundson, Amber and Ryan Amundson 2001: 'Our Grief is not a Cry for War' to Conference, Medford Mass., USA, 7–8 December 2001. http:www.afsc.org/nero/pesp/amundson.htm

Annan, Kofi 2001: 'Message to the Peoples of the United Nations' (Action for UN Renewal, London). www.action-for-un-renewal.org.uk

Annan, Kofi 1999: Interview in *Irish Times*, 23 January 1999, by Mark Brennock: 'Talking of Peace but with Conflict on his Mind'; see also Editorial in same issue.

Arkin, William 2000: 'Preparing the Unthinkable: The United States Nuclear Posture Review', *The Spokesman* No. 75, pp. 52–55.

Atkeson, Edward B. (Brig. Gen., retired): 'Civilian-based Defence and the Art of War', delivered 25 May 1985 and reported in Vogele, W.

Barratt Brown, Michael 2002: *The Third Way... or Feeding the Fat Cats* (Nottingham).

Benn, Tony 2002: 'The Laughter of Our Children', Opening Address to ENHPR Launch Conference, in *The Spokesman*, No. 74, pp. 10–13.

Bennis, Phyllis 1994: 'Blue Helmets – For What? Under Whom?' in Childers, ed., pp. 152–75.

Blackaby, Frank 1996: *Europe and NATO Expansion* (Nottingham).

Bonde, Jens-Peter MEP 2001: *Nice Treaty Explained* with Preface by Romano Prodi (Denmark). www.bonde.dk

Brennan, Mary 2000: 'European Security – Choices, Threats and Opportunities'. Paper for First Consultation, European Network for Peace and Human Rights, Brussels, May 2000.

Bruton, John T.D. 2002: (Rapporteur) Joint Committee on European Affairs, *Report on the Future of the European Union* (Dublin) ['Bruton Report']

Butler, Lee 1999: (Gen., retired) 'Death by Deterrence', *Resurgence*, No. 19, March/April 1999, pp. 7–10.

Caryl, Christian 2002: 'Tyrants on the Take', in *New York Review of Books*, 11 April 2002, pp. 27–30.

Chesterman, Simon and Michael Byers 1999: 'Has US Power Destroyed the UN?', in *London Review of Books*, 29 April 1999, pp. 29–30.

Childers, Erskine 1994: (ed.) *Challenges to the United Nations: Building a Safer World* (London).

Childers, Erskine 1994: 'The United Nations System', in Childers (ed.), pp. 14–25.

Childers, Erskine 1995: 'The Changing Role of the United Nations', paper presented to Department of Foreign Affairs Seminar on the UN, for White Paper on Foreign Policy, University College Cork, 11 March 1995.

Chipp, Beverley 2001: *Going to Court Not War* (London).

Chomsky, Noam 2001: Address to Conference 'After September 11: Paths to Peace, Justice and Security', 7–8 December 2001, Medford, Mass., USA. www.afsc.org/nero/pesp/chomsky.htm

CMRS 1987: (Conference of Major Religious Superiors – now renamed CORI – Conference of Religious in Ireland), *Single European Act Briefing* (Dublin).

Coates, Ken 2000: 'NATO and the New World Disorder', *The Spokesman*, No. 67, pp. 31–42.

Coates, Ken 2002a: 'Power Play and the New World Chaos', ENHPR Launch Conference, *Multilingual Conference Reader*, pp. 1–5.

Coates, Ken 2002b: 'Peace and Human Rights are Overdue: Why We Need a European Network for Peace and Human Rights', *The Spokesman*, No. 74, pp. 5–9.

Cowen, Brian TD 2002: National Forum on Europe, Report of Plenary Session, *EU Common Foreign Policy and Security 21 February 2002*, p. 56 (Dublin).

Cullen Owens, Rosemary 2001: *Louie Bennett* (Cork).

ENHPR 2002: 'Communiqué of the Founding Conference of the European Network for Peace and Human Rights' Brussels, 1 February 2002, *The Spokesman*, No. 74, pp. 16–17. elfeuro@compuserve.com

EU 1997: Treaty of Amsterdam (Luxembourg).

EU 1999: Presidency Conclusions, Berlin European Council 24/25 March 1999: *Statement by the European Council Concerning the Kosovo*.

EU 2000: Council Presidency Report 'European Security and Defence Policy' (November 2000) for Nice Summit, December 2000.

EU 2001: *The Future of the European Union – Laeken Declaration 15th December 2001*, in Bruton, pp. 76–85.

Farebrother, George 2000: *A New Agenda for NATO* (Abolition 2000 UK, London).

Fianna Fail 1997: *Election Manifesto*, p. 133.

Forsberg, Randall 1994: 'Wasting Billions', *Boston Review*, April-May 1994. http://www.boston review.mit.edu/BR19.2/forsberg.html

Gallagher, Eamonn 2002: Remarks to National Forum on Europe, *Hearing of Presentations, Based on Submissions Received, 31 January 2002*, Report of Proceedings No. 9 (Dublin).

Gallagher, Eamonn and John Temple Lang 2002: 'What sort of European Commission does the European Union need?', presentation to National Forum on Europe, 31 January 2002. www.actioncentreeurope.org.uk/publications/whatsortofcommission/printable.html, accessed 20 June 2002.

Gerson, Joseph 2002A: 'Roots of the War, Roots of Resistance' in ENHPR Launch Conference, *3rd Conference Reader*.

Gerson, Joseph 2002B: 'Roots of War, Roots of Resistance', 1/29 Draft. www.afsc.org/pes.htm

Giddens, Anthony 1999, *Runaway World: Reith Lectures 1999*; Lecture V: 'Democratising Democracy' text from BBC Homepage, accessed summer 1999.

Giddens, Anthony 2002: *Where Now for New Labour?* Fabian Society Pamphlet (London).

Glennon, Michael J. 2001: *Limits of Law, Prerogatives of Power: Interventionism after Kosovo* (New York).

Gourevitch, Philip 1999: *We wish to inform you that tomorrow we will be killed with our families* (London).

Halliday, Denis and Hans von Sponeck 2001: 'The Hostage Nation', *Guardian*, 29 January 2001.

Harbottle, Brig. Michael 1996: *Open Letter* (December 1996).

Hayes, Senator Maurice 2002a: National Forum on Europe – Chairman's Report, *The First Phase of Work*. www.forumoneurope.ie

Hayes, Senator Maurice 2002b: National Forum on Europe – Chairman's Report, *The Second Phase of Work*.

Hyland, Tom 2000: 'Lessons for the United Nations to Learn from East Timor' in *'Transforming the United Nations' Conference* (PANA/UNICEF/Irish United Nations Association, Dublin).

134 BIBLIOGRAPHY

IICK 2000: (Independent International Commission on Kosovo) *Kosovo Report* (2000).

IPU 2002: (Irish Pharmaceutical Union) Leaflet, 'Prescription for Disaster' (Dublin).

Ireland 1986: *The Single European Act: An Explanatory Guide* (Dublin).

Ireland 1996: *Challenges and Opportunities Abroad – White Paper on Foreign Policy* (Dublin).

Ireland 1998: *Treaty of Amsterdam: White Paper* (Dublin).

Ireland 1999a: *Ireland and the Partnership for Peace: An Explanatory Guide* (Dublin). http://www.irlgov.ie/iveagh

Ireland 1999b: *Bunreacht na hÉireann*.

Ireland 2000: *White Paper on Defence* (Dublin).

Ireland 2001: *Treaty of Nice: White Paper* (Dublin).

Keatinge, Patrick and Ben Tonra 2002: *The European Rapid Reaction Force*, (Institute of European Affairs, Dublin). www.iiea.com

Kennan, George 1999: Richard Ullman 'The US and the World: An Interview with George Kennan', *New York Review of Books*, 12 August 1999, pp. 4–6.

Kenny, Karen 2001: 'Ireland, the Security Council and Afghanistan: Promoting or Undermining the International Rule of Law?', in *Trócaire Development Review*, 2001, pp. 101–28.

Lewis, JAC 2000: 'Europe to Provide Troops for Rapid Reaction Force', *Jane's Defence Weekly*, 17 November 2000, p. 1. www.Janes.com/defence/news/jdw001122_01_n.shtml

McLean, Andrew 1999: 'Stemming the Deadly Flow'. http://www.vso.org.uk./pubs/orbit/orbit/60/arms.htm, accessed July 1999.

Maguire, John 1999: *Defending Peace: For an Alternative to NATO/PfP and a Militarised Europe* (Cork and Dublin).

Maguire, John 2002: Presentation to National Forum on Europe Plenary Session, *EU Common Foreign Policy and Security*, 21 February 2002.

Maguire, John and Joe Noonan 1992: *Maastricht and Neutrality: Ireland's Neutrality and the Future of Europe* (Cork).

Moeller, Bjoern edits *NOD and Conversion* for the Copenhagen Peace Research Institute, 1985 onwards.

National Platform 2002: 'Additional Submission' to National Forum on Europe, 13 March 2002. www.nationalplatform.org

BIBLIOGRAPHY 135

NATO 1999: *NATO Handbook 50th Anniversary Edition* (Brussels).

Nobel Peace Laureates 2001: 'Statement by 8 Nobel Peace Prize Laureates', in *IPB News: Newsletter of the International Peace Bureau* (Dec. 2001), p. 7. www.ipb.org

O'Kennedy, Michael T.D. 1999: 'Dail Statement on Partnership for Peace Motion', Thursday, 28 January 1999.

Oxford Research Group 2001: *War Prevention Works: 50 Stories of People Resolving Conflict* ed. Dylan Mathews (Oxford) <org@oxfordresearchgroup.org.uk>.

PANA 1998: (Peace and Neutrality Alliance), *The Amsterdam Treaty: From Positive Neutrality to Nuclear Insanity* (Dublin). pana@eircom.net

PANA 1999: *The PfP Road from Neutrality to NATO and the WEU* (Dublin).

Peace Matters, No. 36, Winter 2001/02, pp. 8–9: 'Good Deeds'.

Perugia 2001: 4th Assembly of the Peoples' United Nations, *Final Document*: 'Globalisation from Below: The Role of Global Civil Society and of Europe' (Perugia, October 2001).

Pilger, John 1989: *Heroes* (London).

Pilger, John 1998: *Hidden Agendas* (London).

Polk, William R. 1999: 'Iraq: A New Leaf', in *New York Review of Books*, 18 February 1999, pp. 34–6.

Regan, Colm 1996: 'Arming Ourselves to Death', in Colm Regan, (ed.) *75:25 – Ireland in an Increasingly Unequal World* (Dublin), pp. 195–208.

Roy, Arundhati 1999: *The Cost of Living* (London).

Rogers, Paul 1995: 'Development, Environment and International Security' paper to 25th Anniversary Conference, Development and Project Planning Centre, University of Bradford, April 1995.

Schell, Jonathan 1998: *The Gift of Time: The Case for Abolishing Nuclear Weapons Now* (London).

Shawcross, William 2000: *Deliver Us from Evil: Warlords and Peacekeepers in a World of Endless Conflict* (London).

Singer, J. David 1986: 'Strategic Deterrence Options: Violent, Nonviolent and Otherwise', presented 26 February 1986 and reported in Vogele.

Skidelsky, Robert 1999: 'The End of National Sovereignty: Kosovo and Blair's New Doctrine of the International Community'. Revised text of a public lecture, London, 14 June 1999.

Storey, Andy 1999: *The Treaty of Nice, NATO and a European Army: Implications for Ireland* (Afri Position Paper No. 3, Dublin).

BIBLIOGRAPHY

Tyler, Jo and Adam Berry (compilers): *Time to Abolish War! A Youth Agenda for Peace and Justice* (Hague Appeal for Peace, Hague, n.d.).

United Nations 1999a: *Report of the Secretary-General pursuant to General Assembly Resolution 53/35: The Fall of Srebrenica* A/54/549 ['Srebrenica Report'].

United Nations 1999b: *Report of the Independent Inquiry into the Actions of the United Nations During the 1994 Genocide in Rwanda* S/1999/1257 ['Carlsson Report'].

United Nations 2000: *Report of the Panel on United Nations Peace Operations* A /55/305 – S /2000/809 ['Brahimi Report'].

United Nations 2001: *Charter of the United Nations and Statute of the International Court of Justice* (New York).

Urquhart, Brian 1999a: 'How Not to Fight a Dictator', in *New York Review of Books*, 6 May 1999, pp. 25–29.

Urquhart, Brian 1999b: 'The Making of a Scapegoat', in *New York Review of Books*, 12 August 1999, pp. 32–35.

Urquhart, Brian 1993: 'For a UN Volunteer Military Force', in *New York Review of Books*, 10 June 1993, pp. 3–4.

US Joint Chiefs of Staff 2002: 'Joint Vision 2020', in *The Spokesman*, No. 74, pp. 58–76.

Vogele, William Report of Seminar Series *Defense, Deterrence and Nonviolent Action*.

http://data.fas.harvard.edu/cfia/pnscs/DOCS/Struggle/defense.htm